FABULOUS FOXES COLORING BOOK

A fox coloring book for kids and adults to enjoy!

www.pretoriuspublishing.com

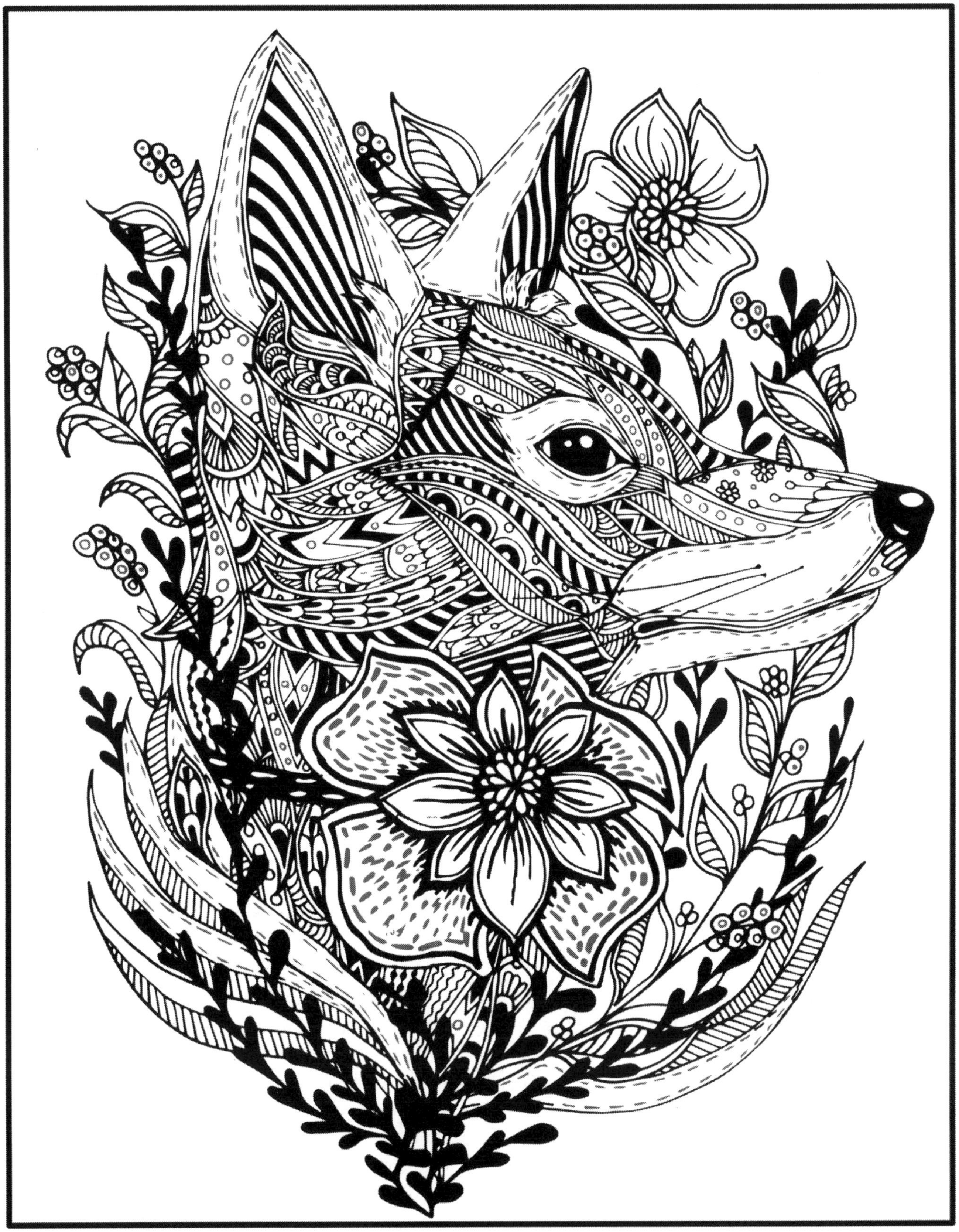

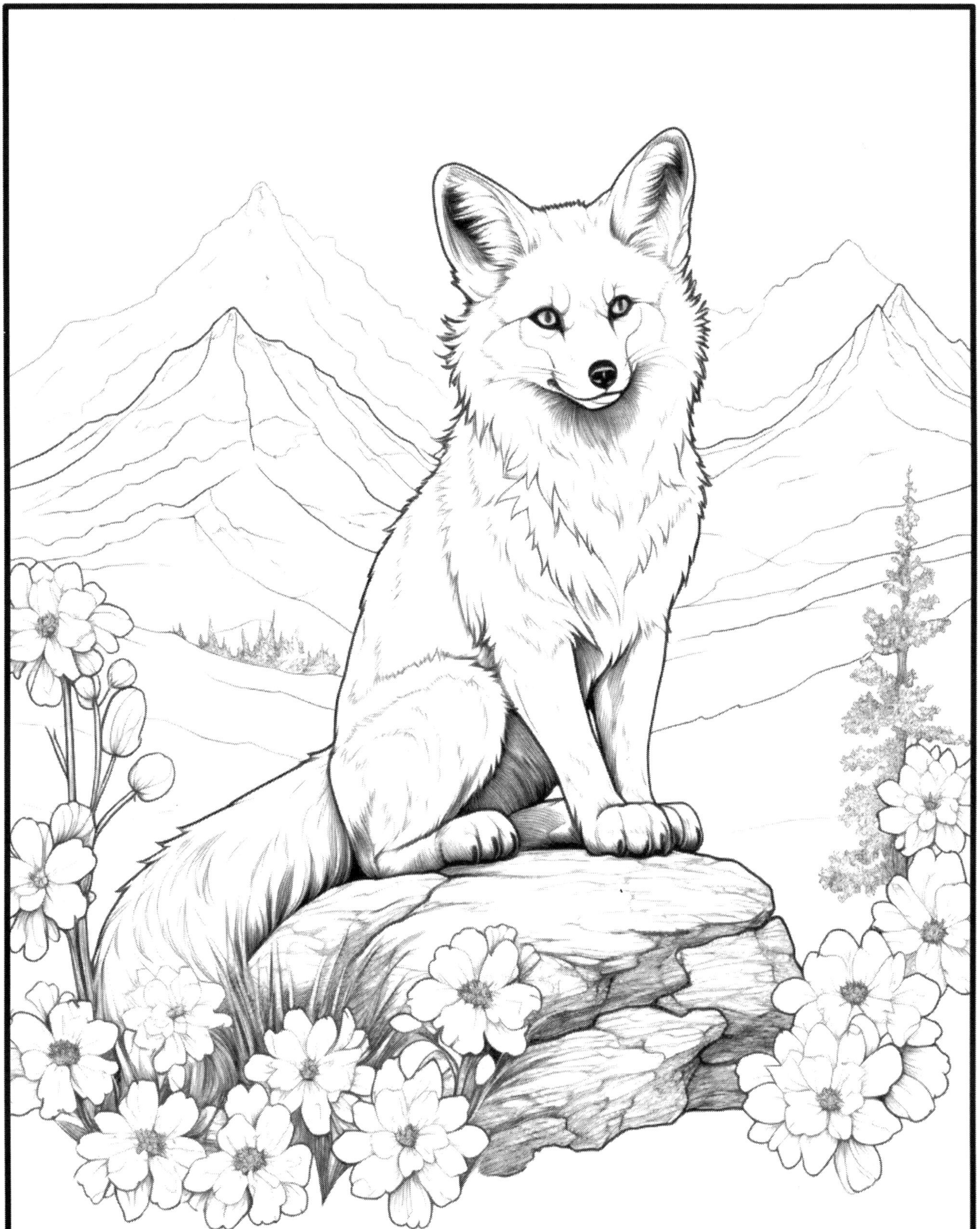

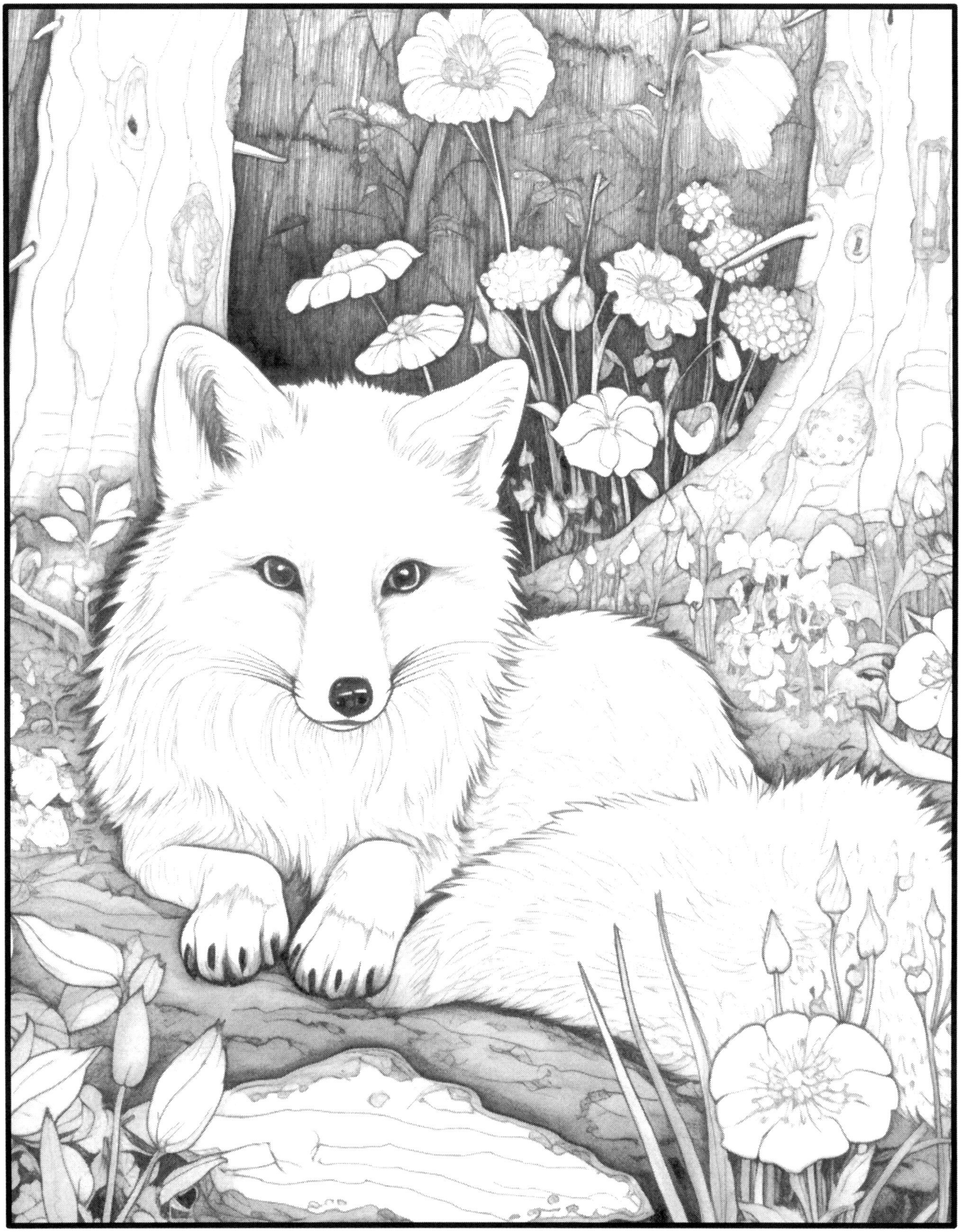

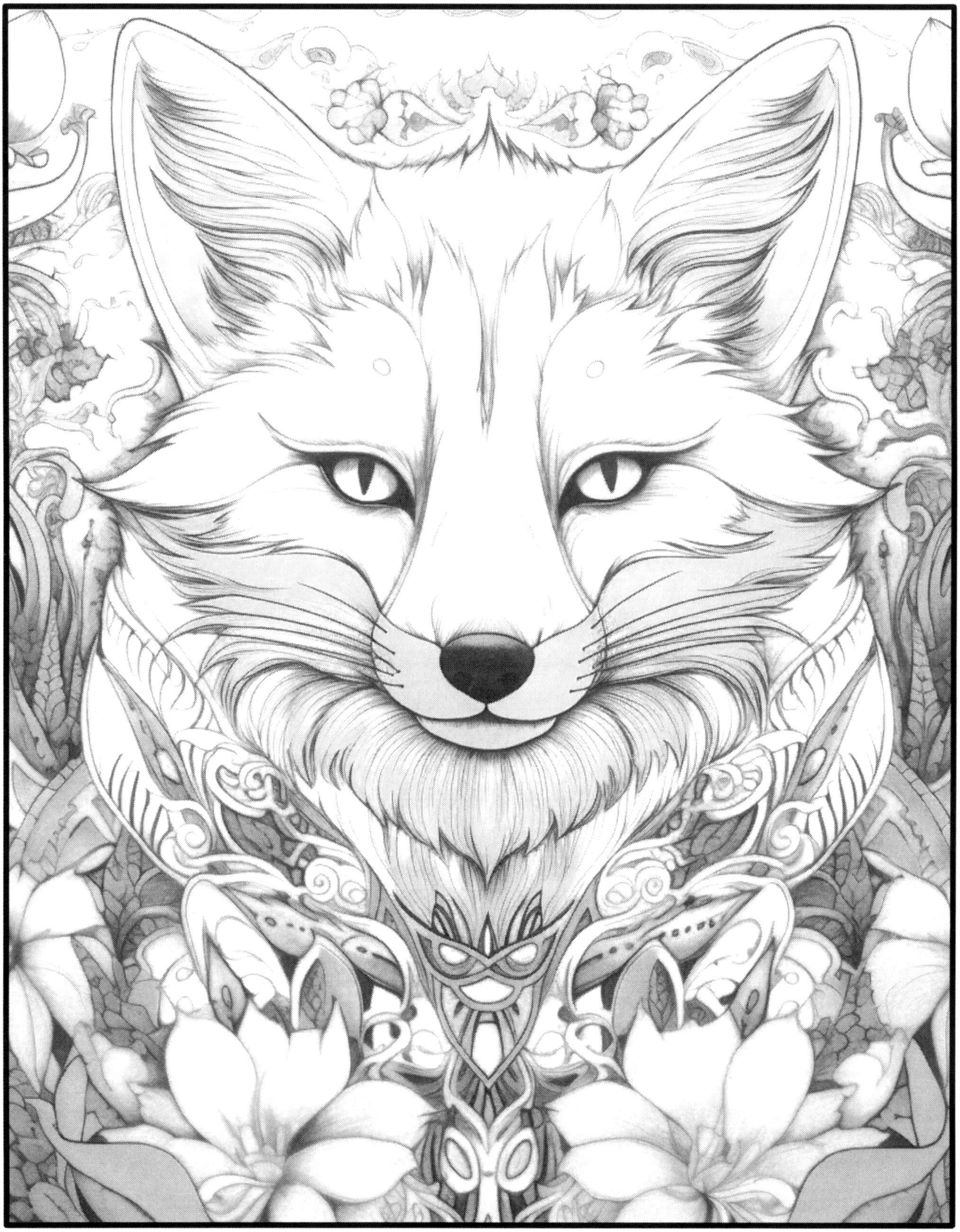

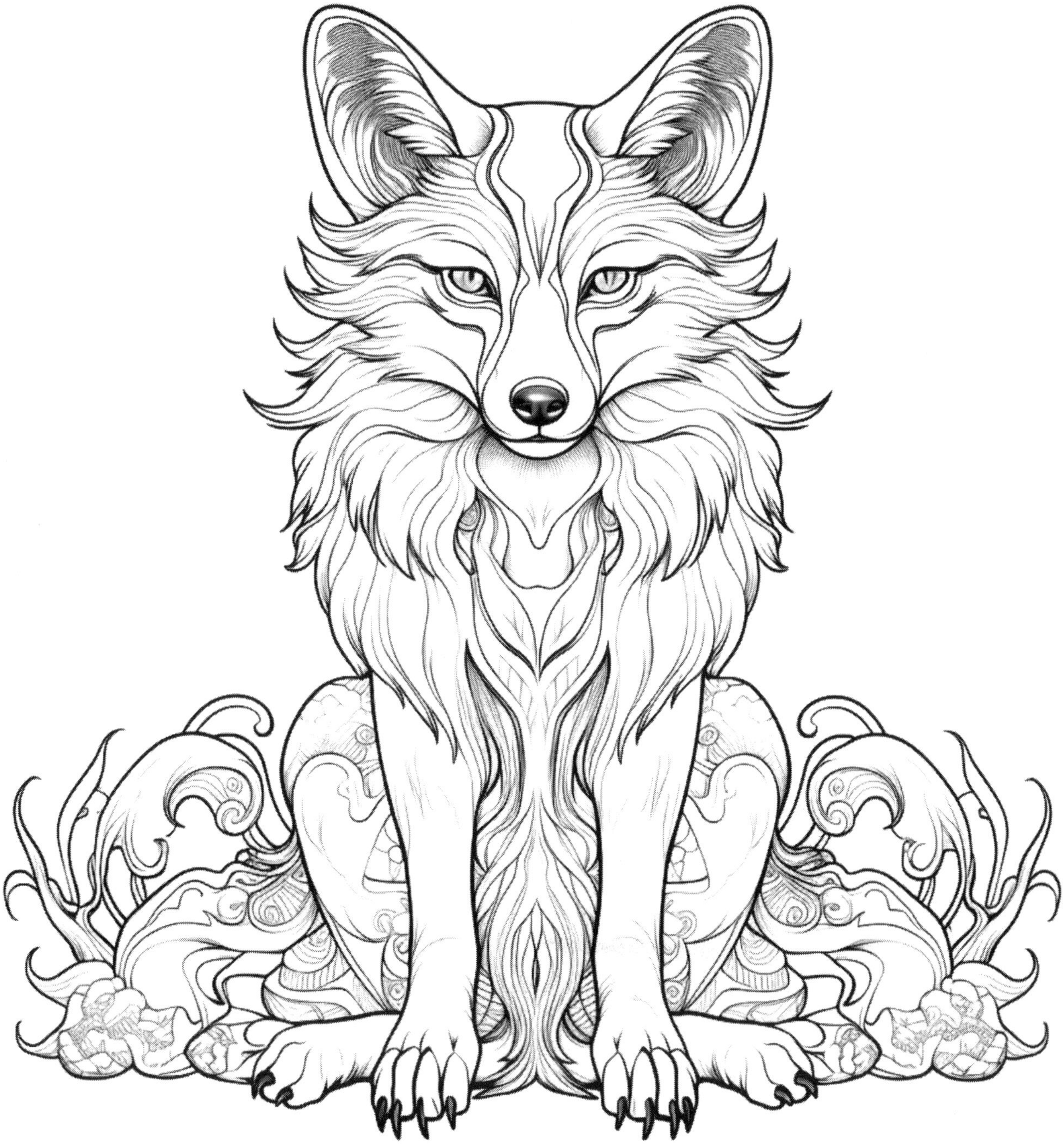

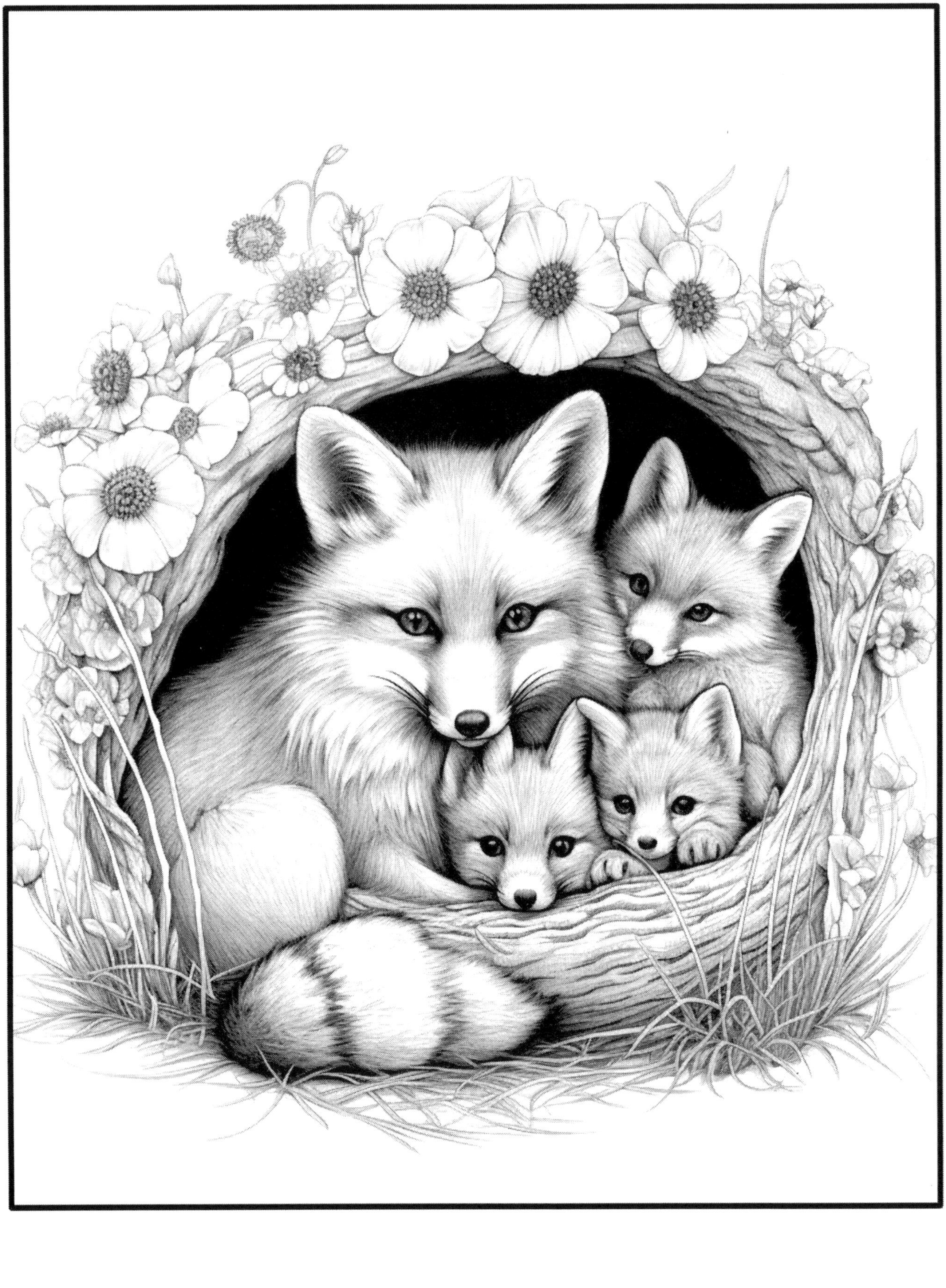

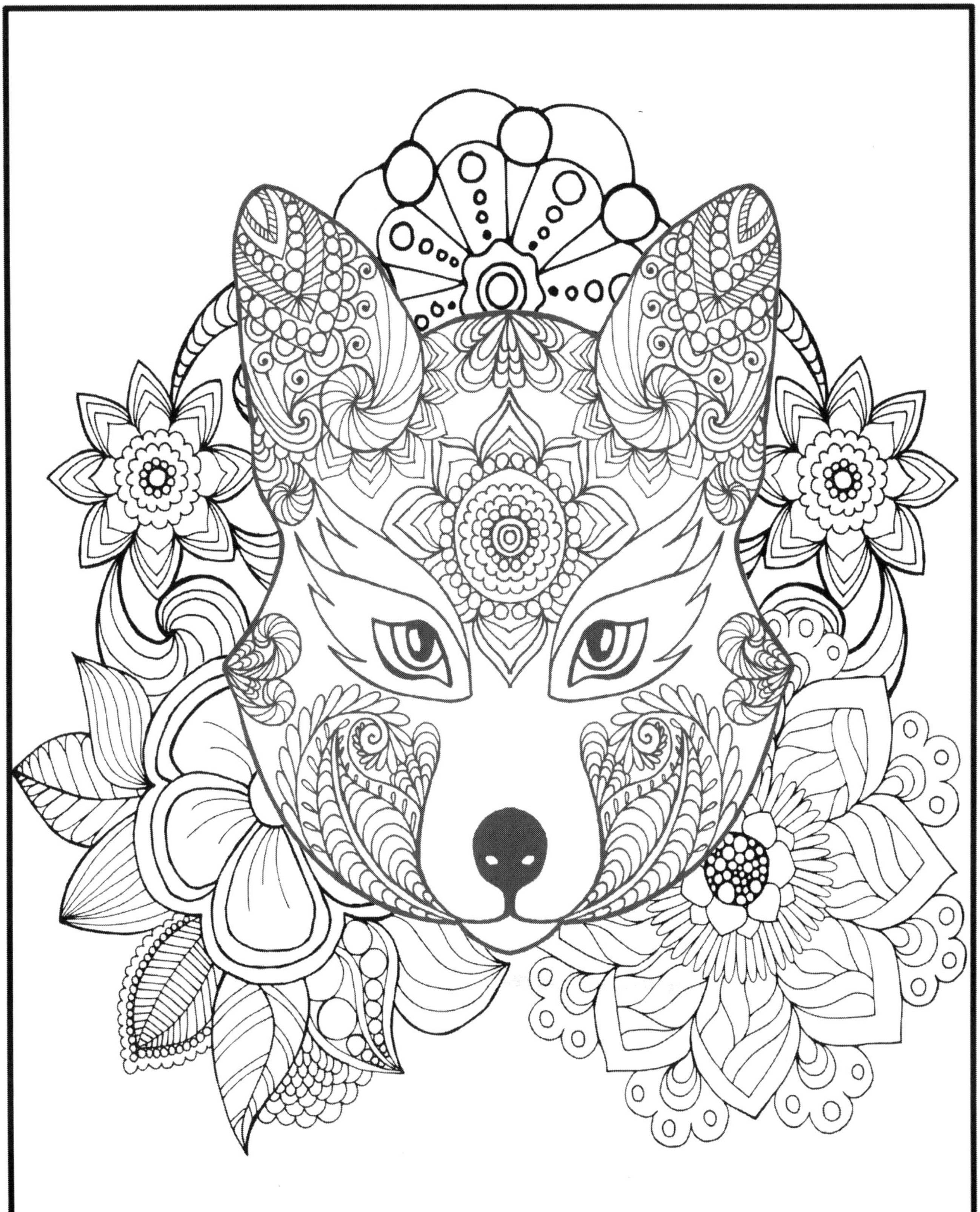

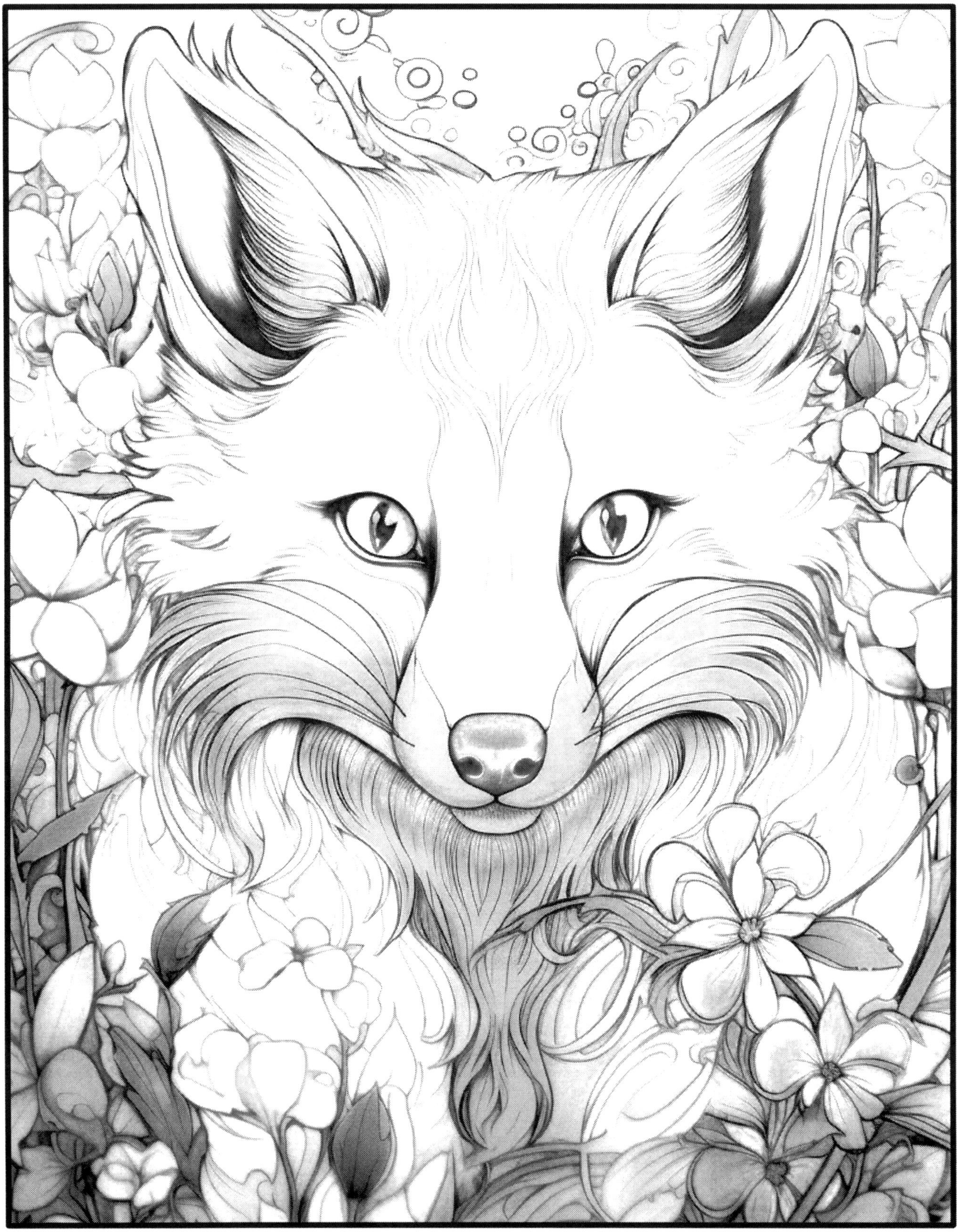

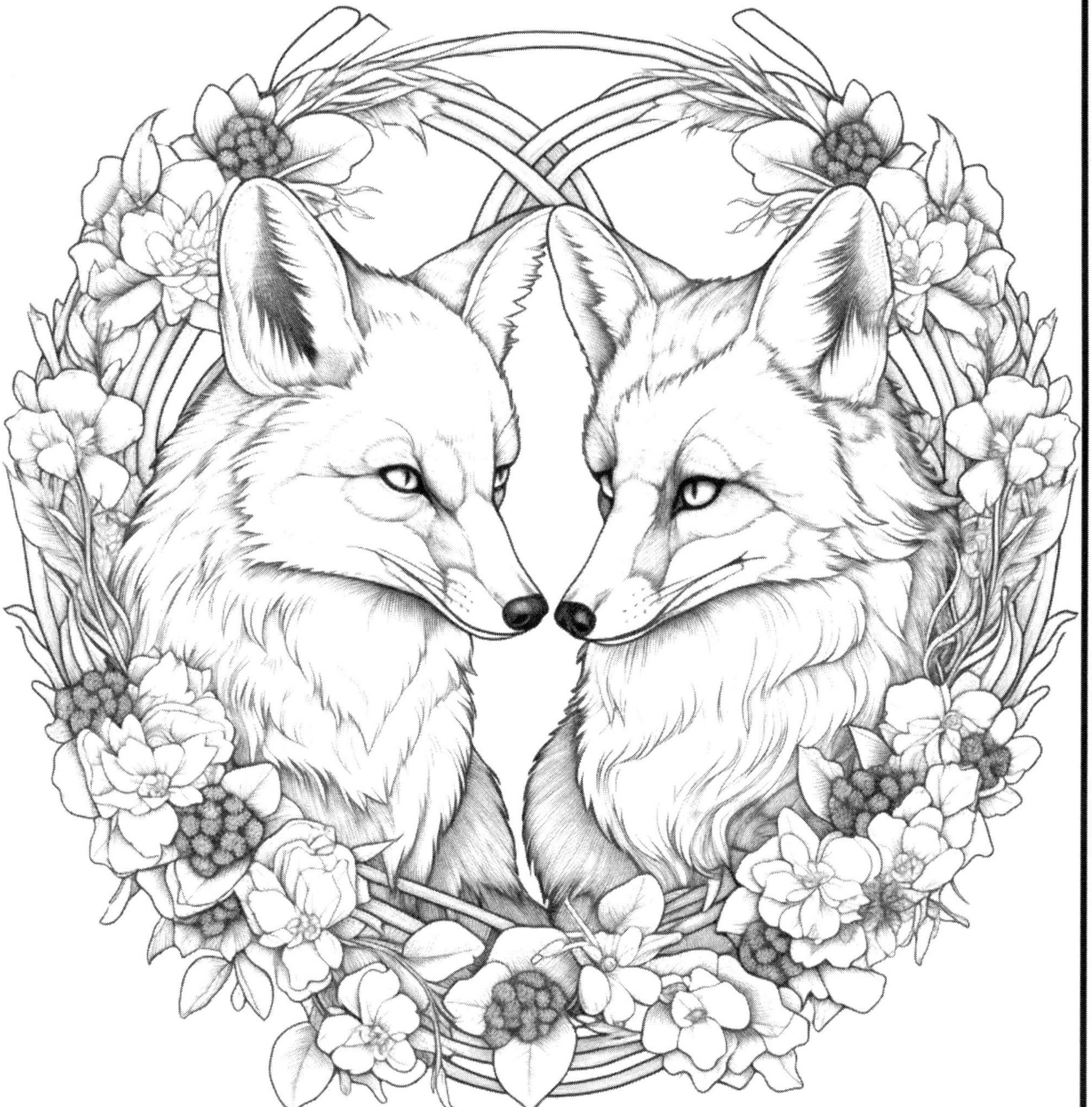

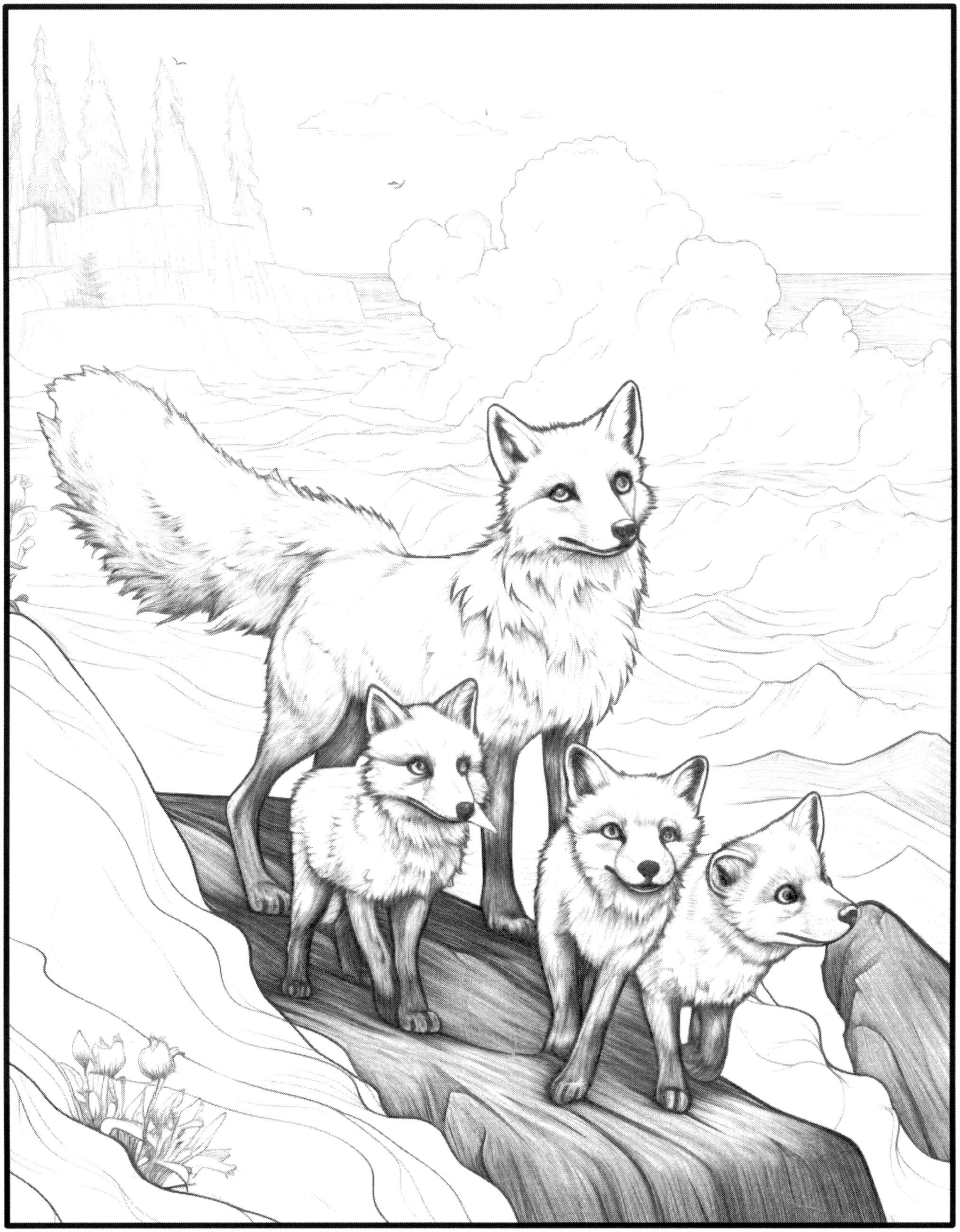

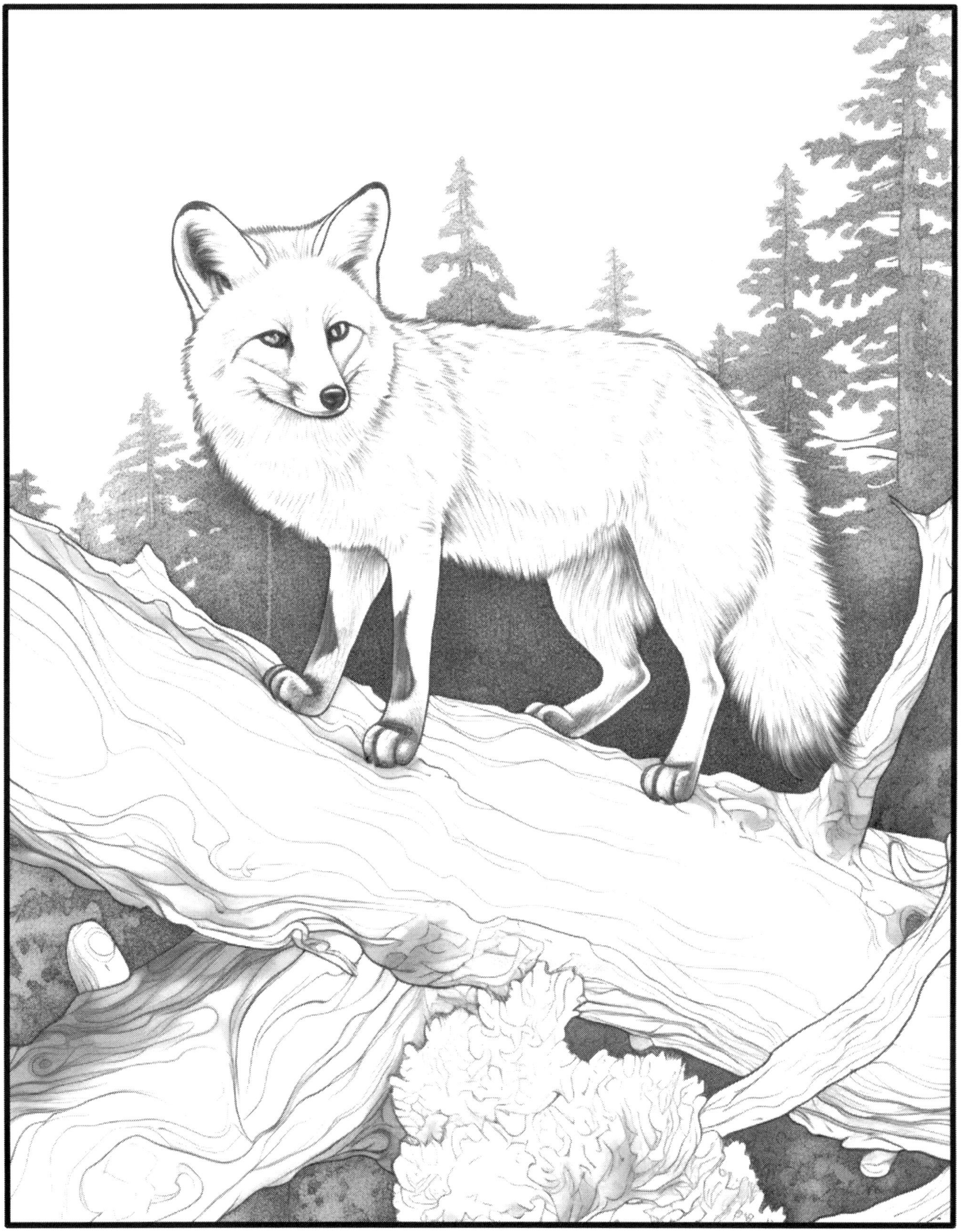

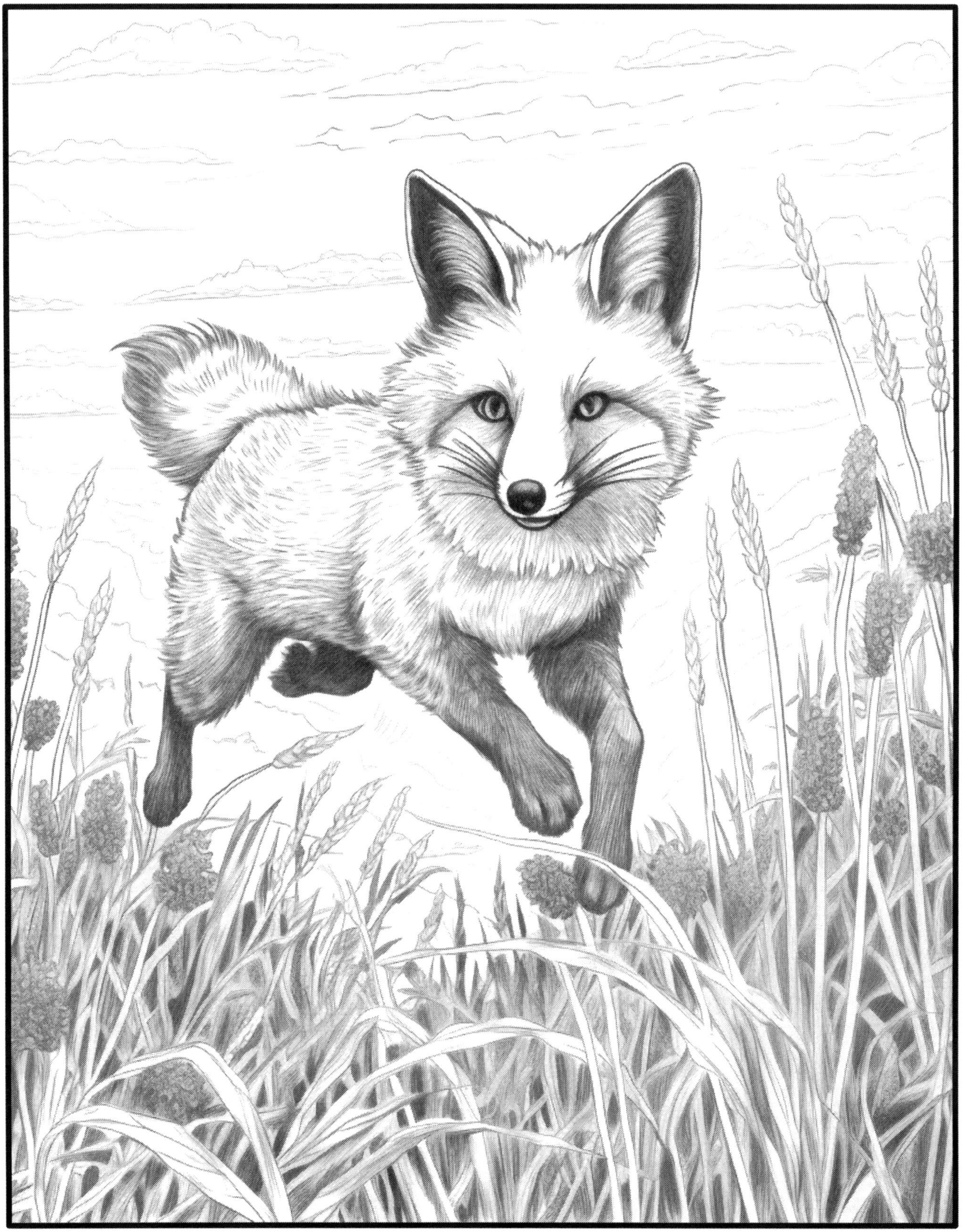

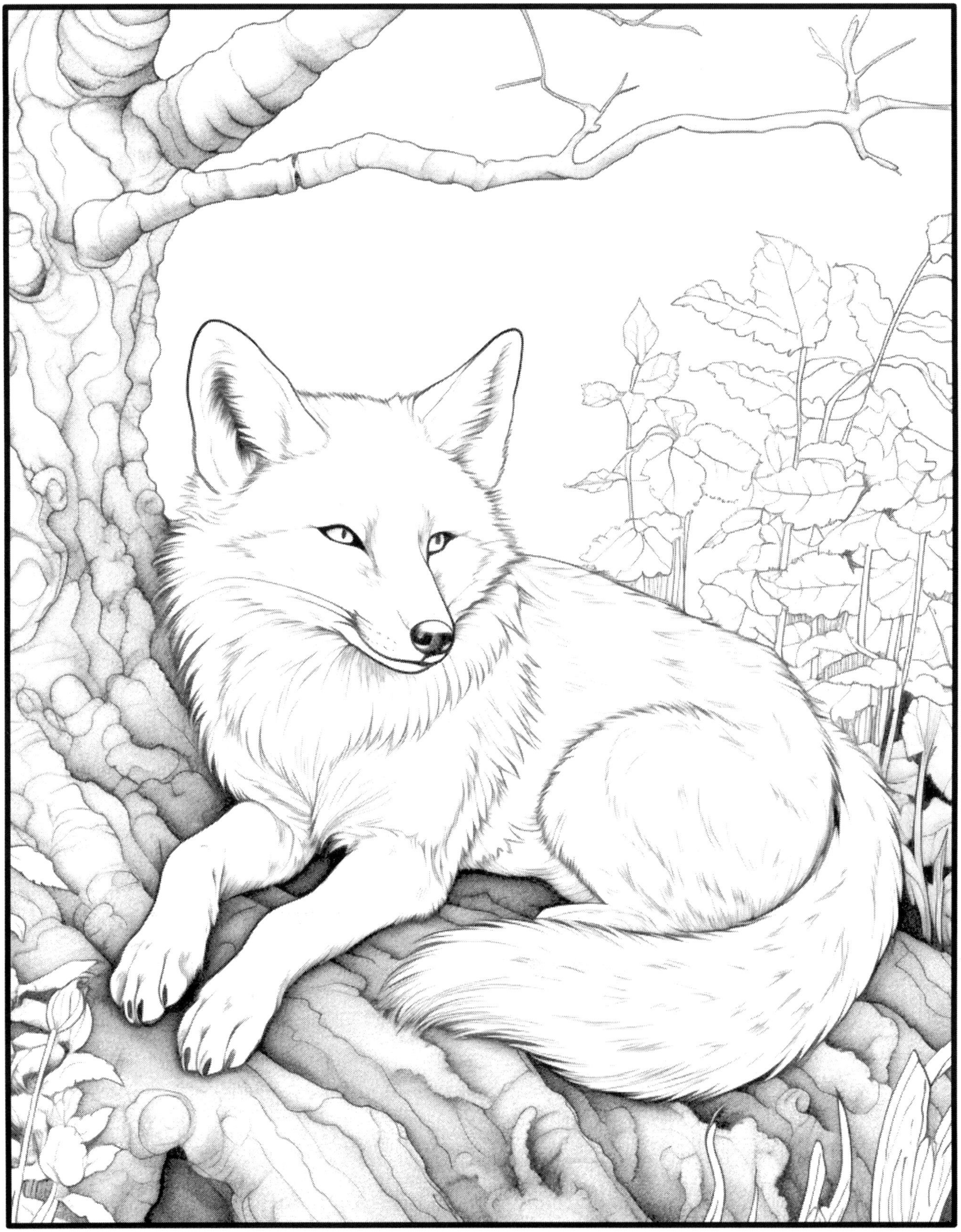

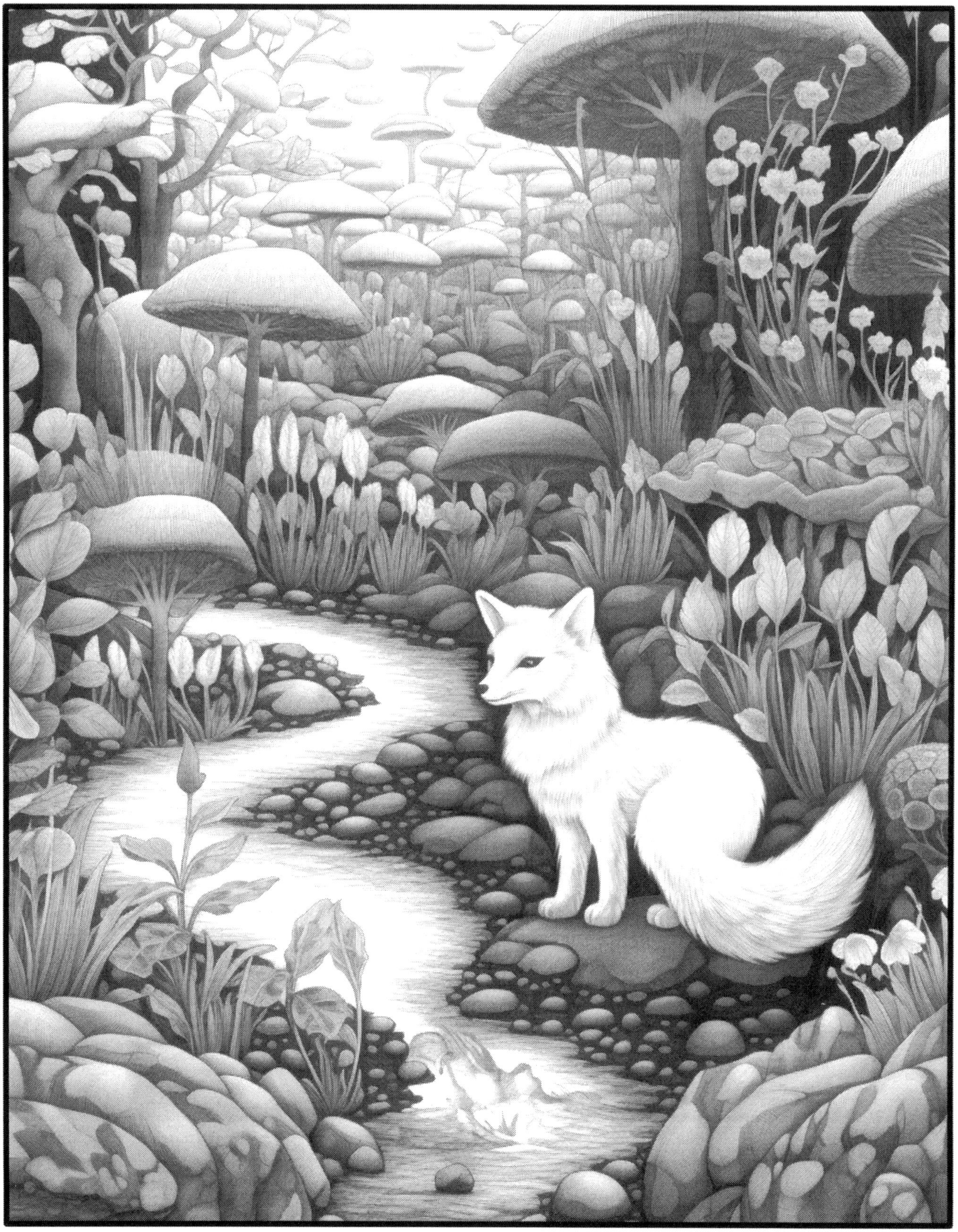

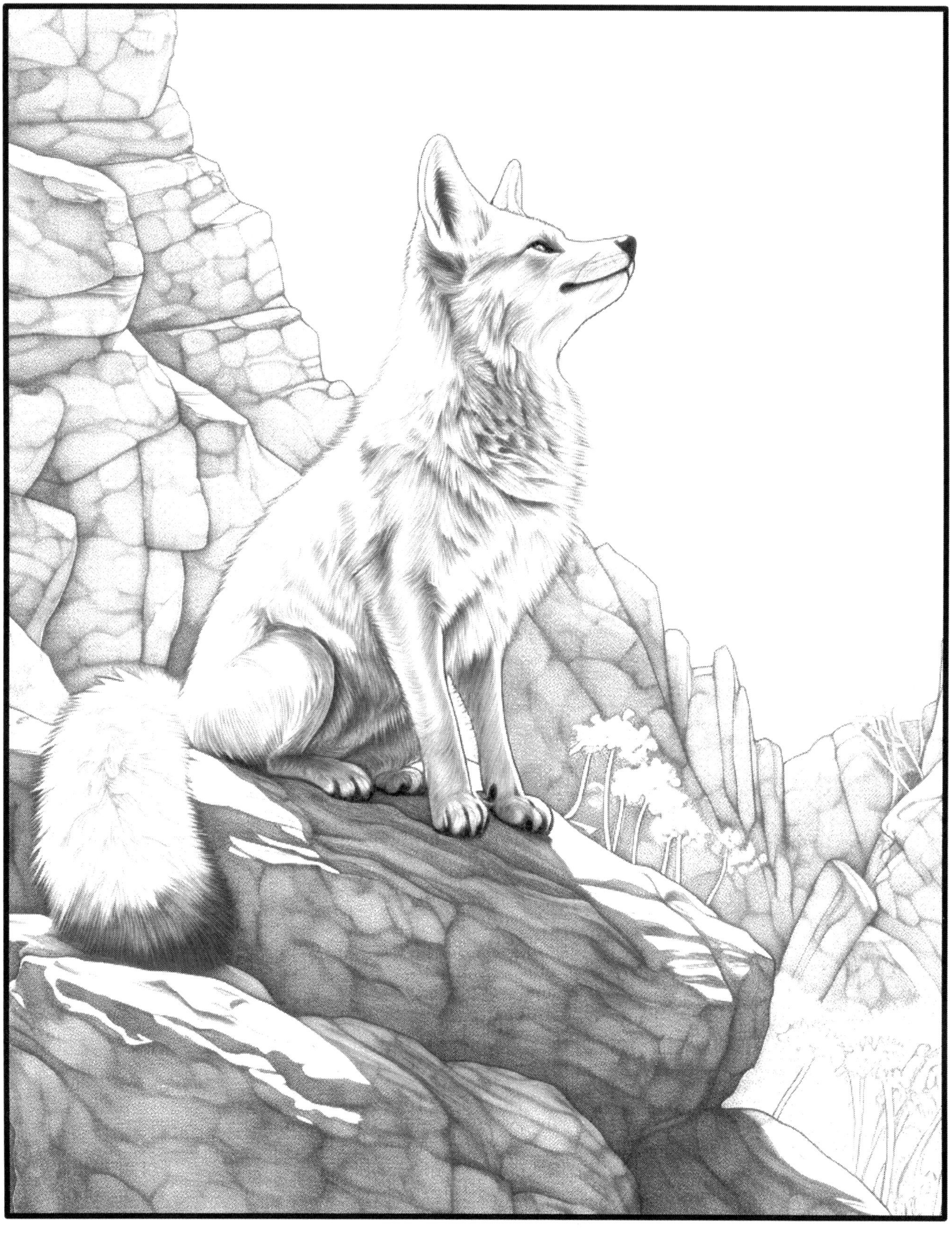

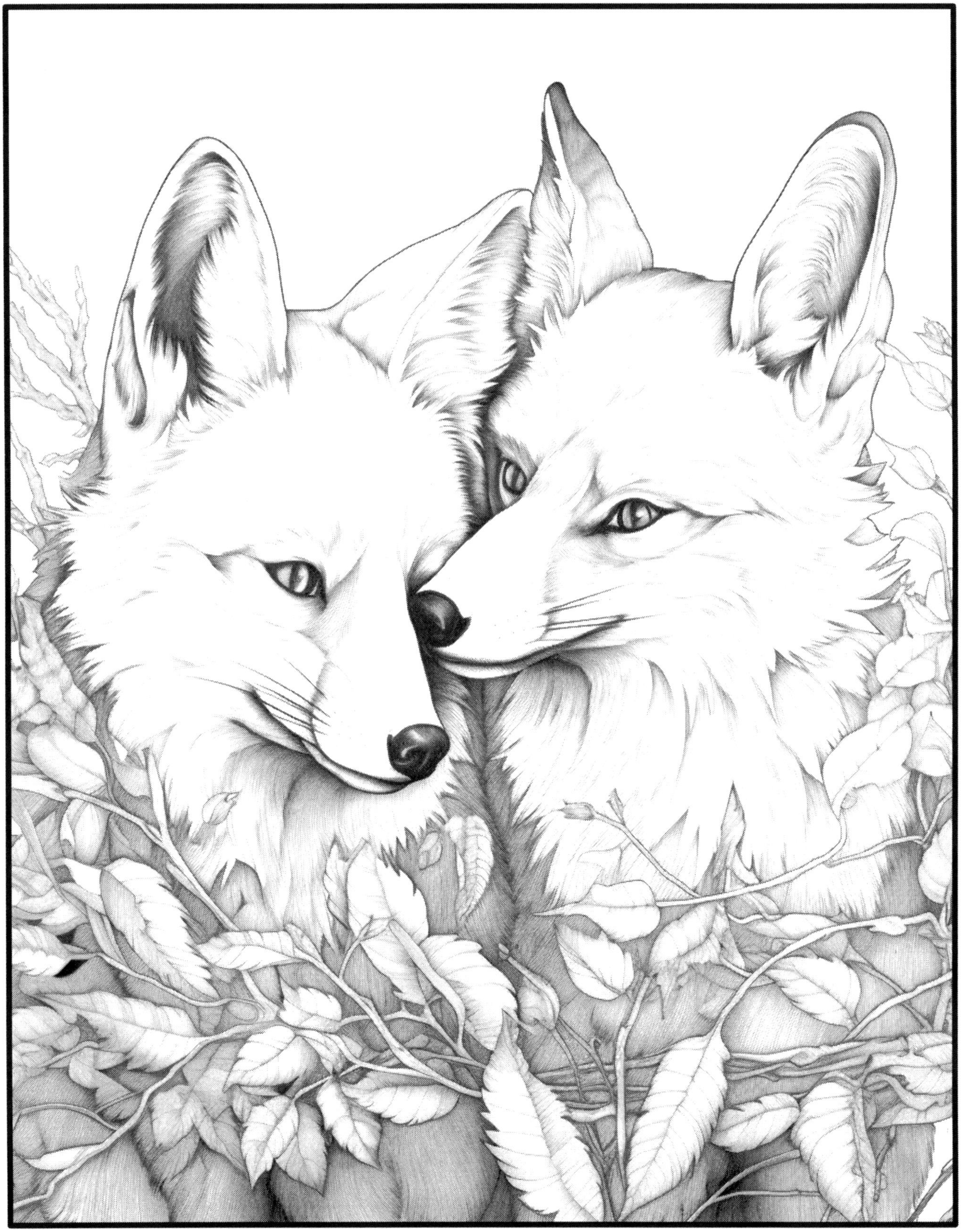

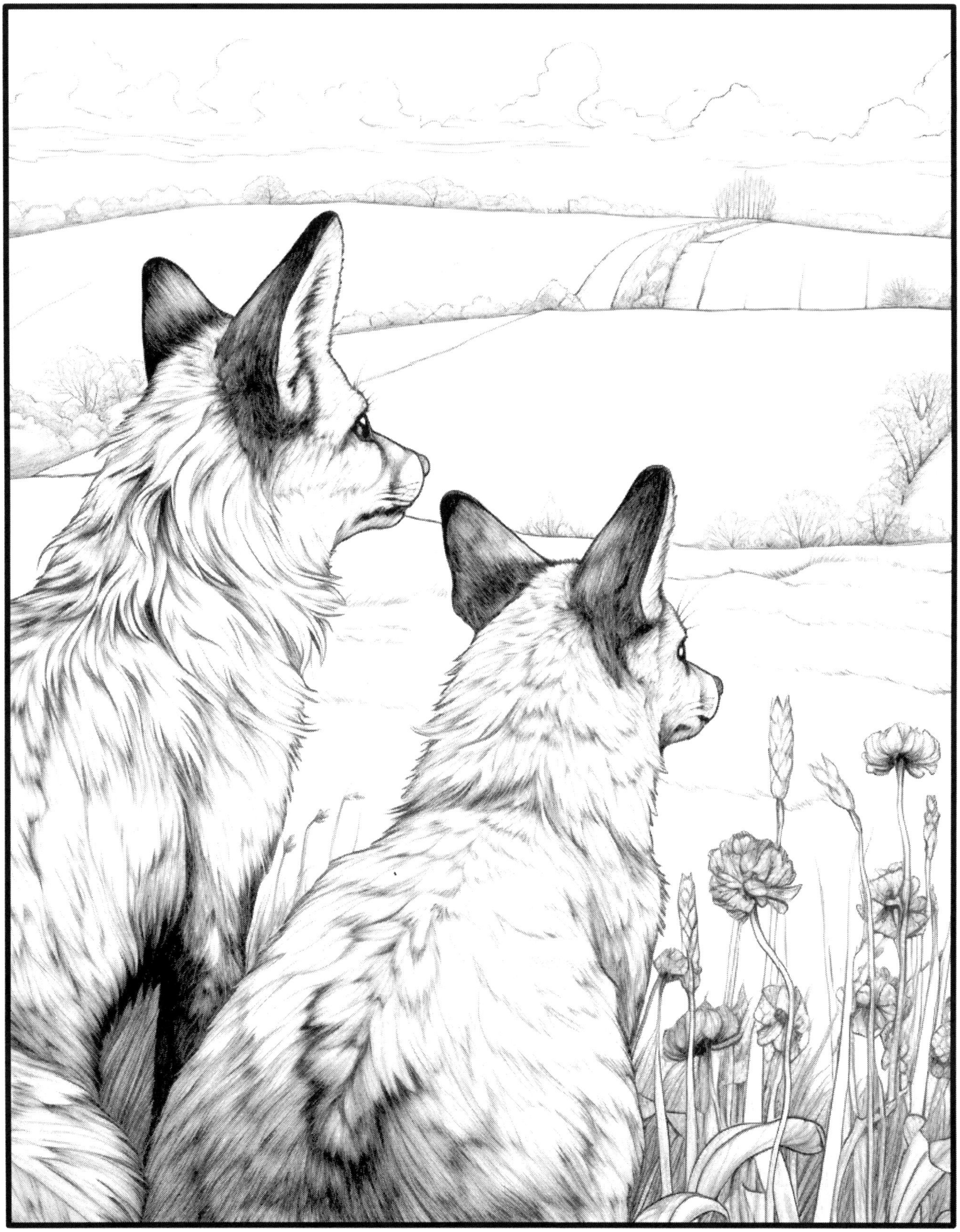

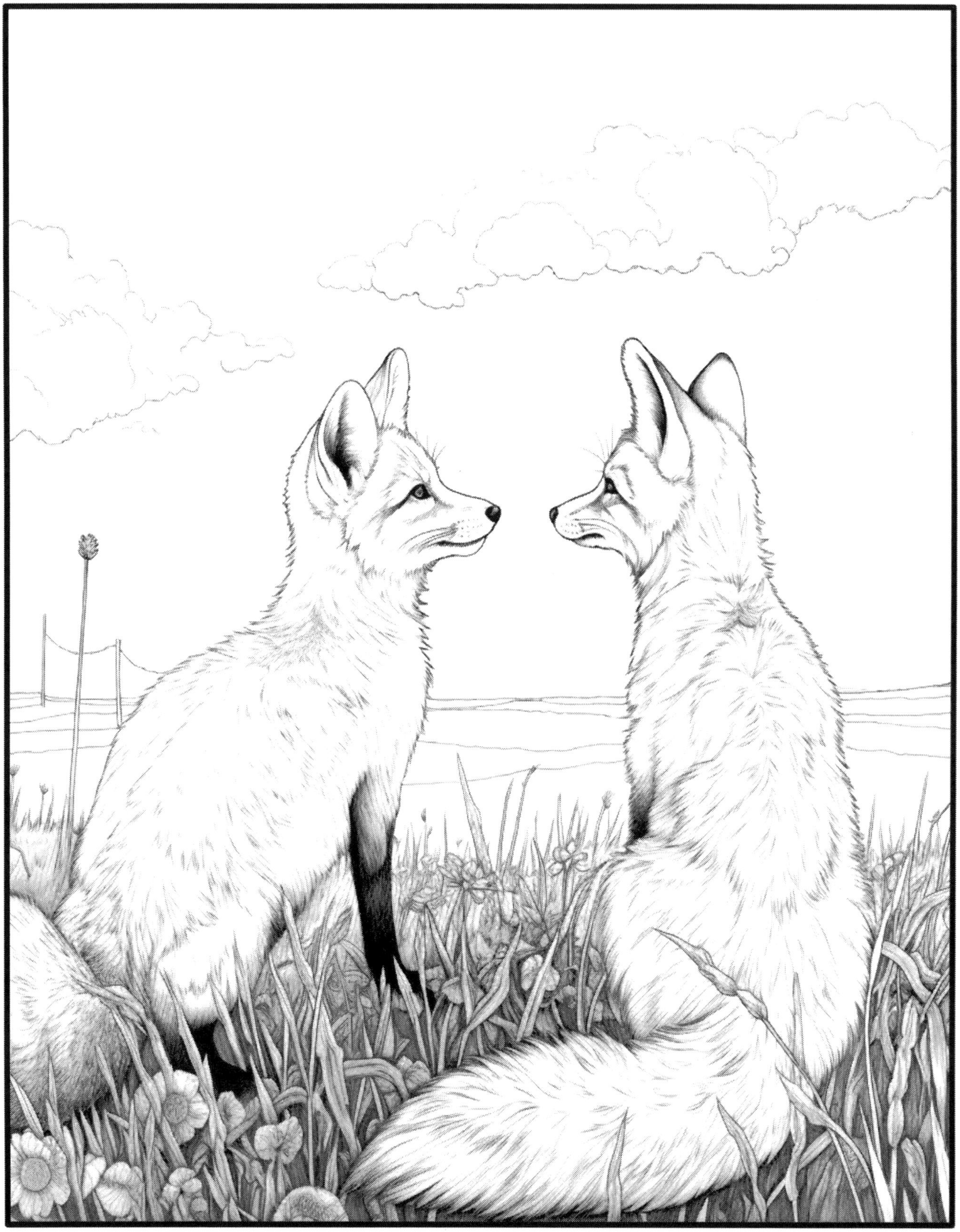

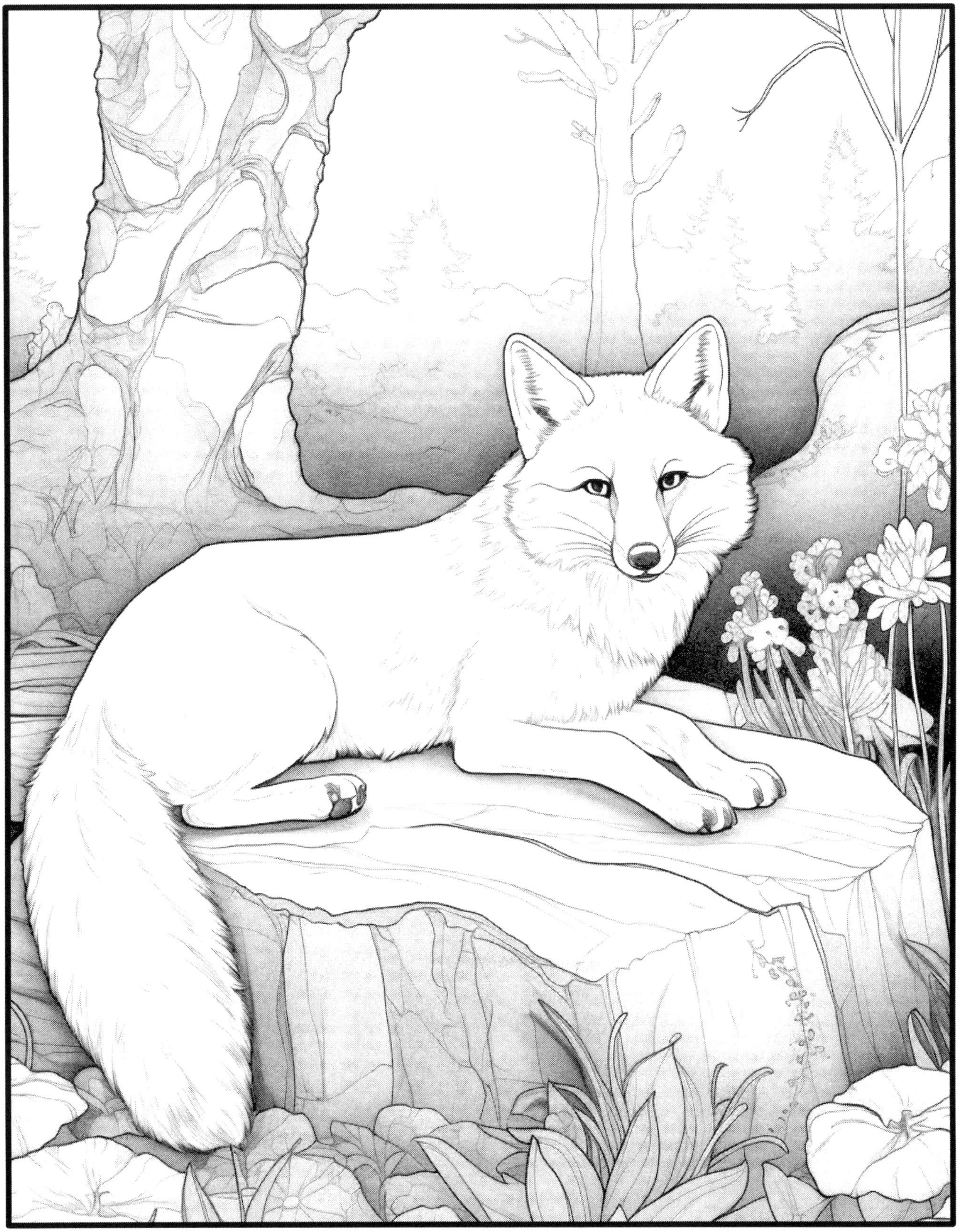

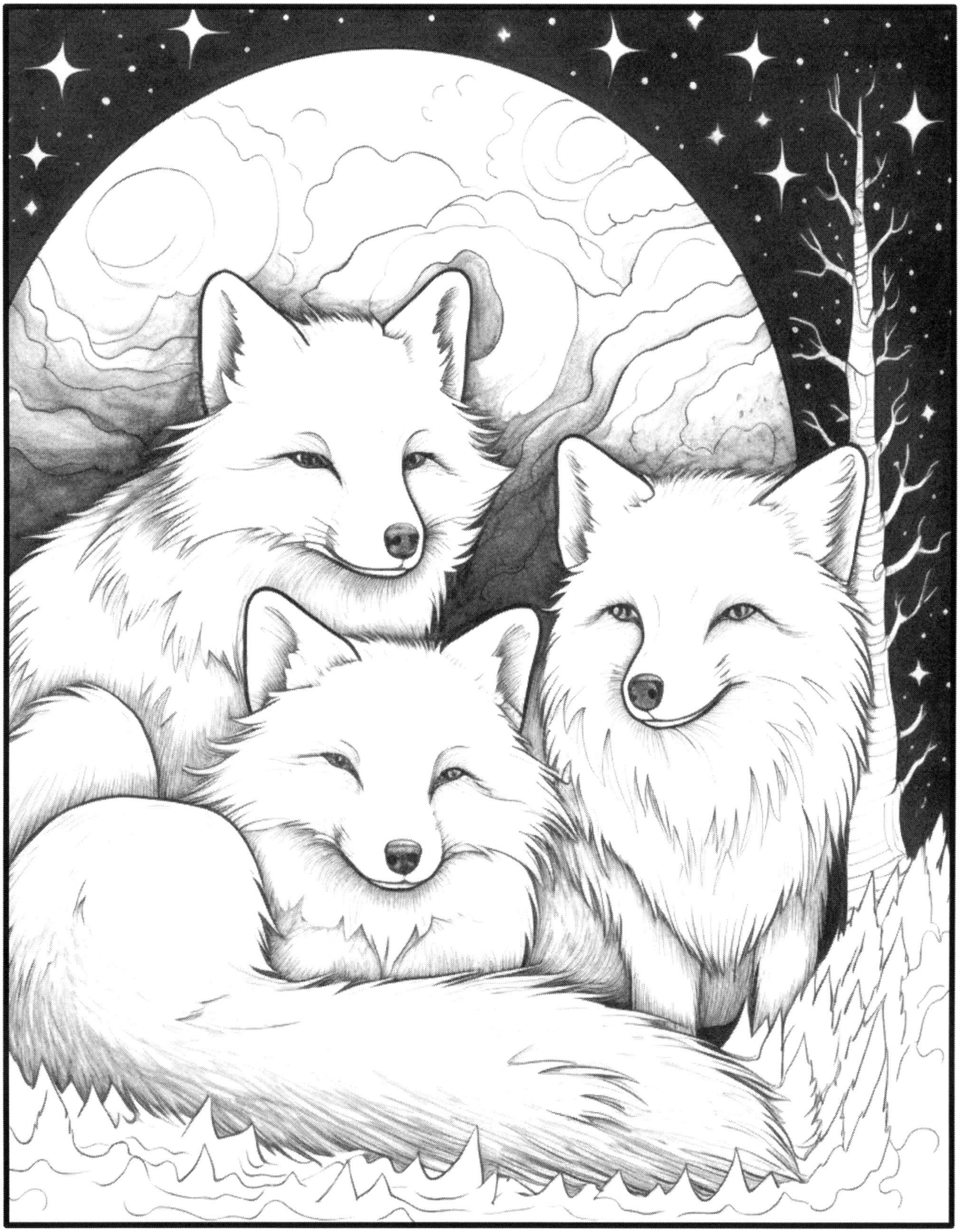

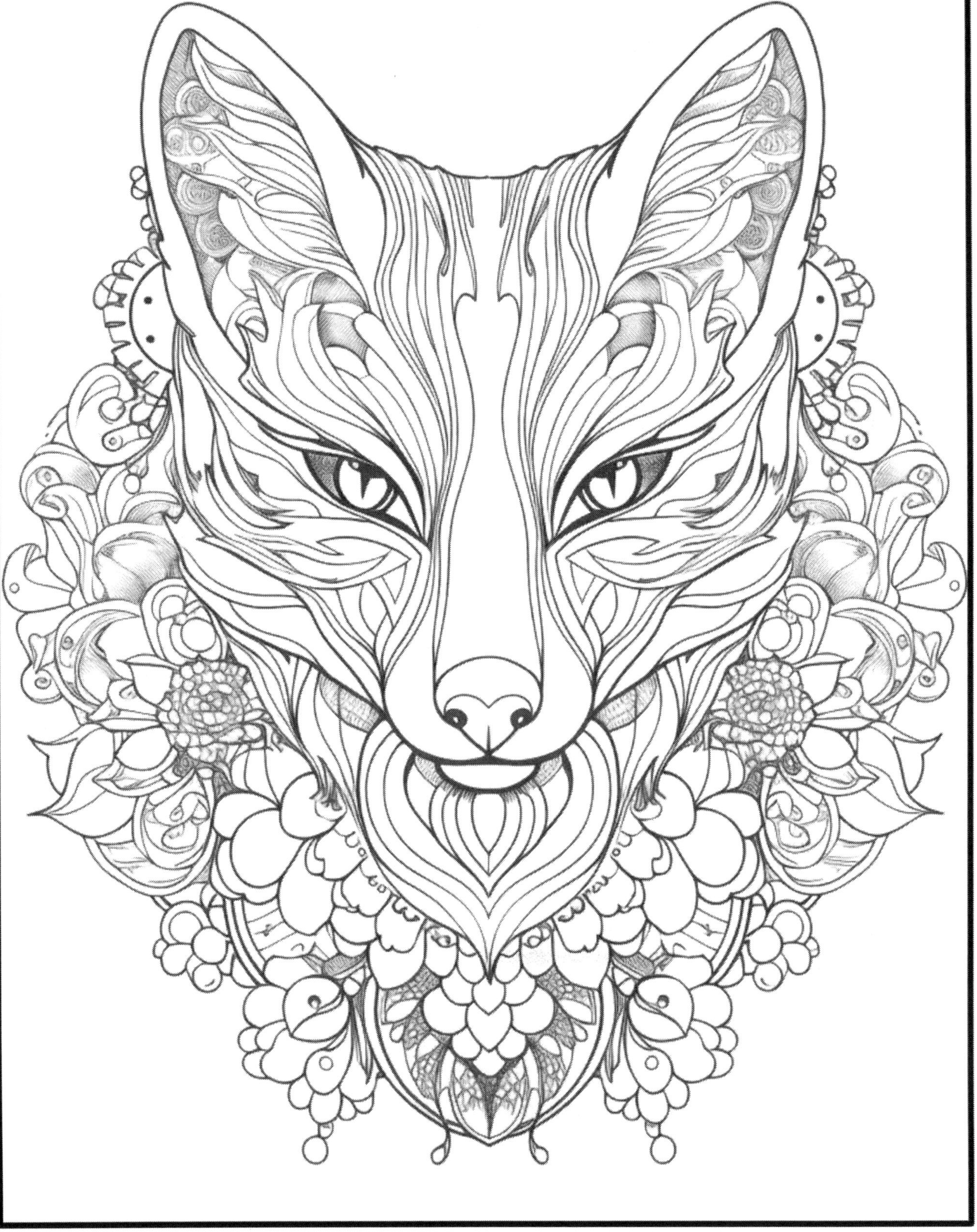

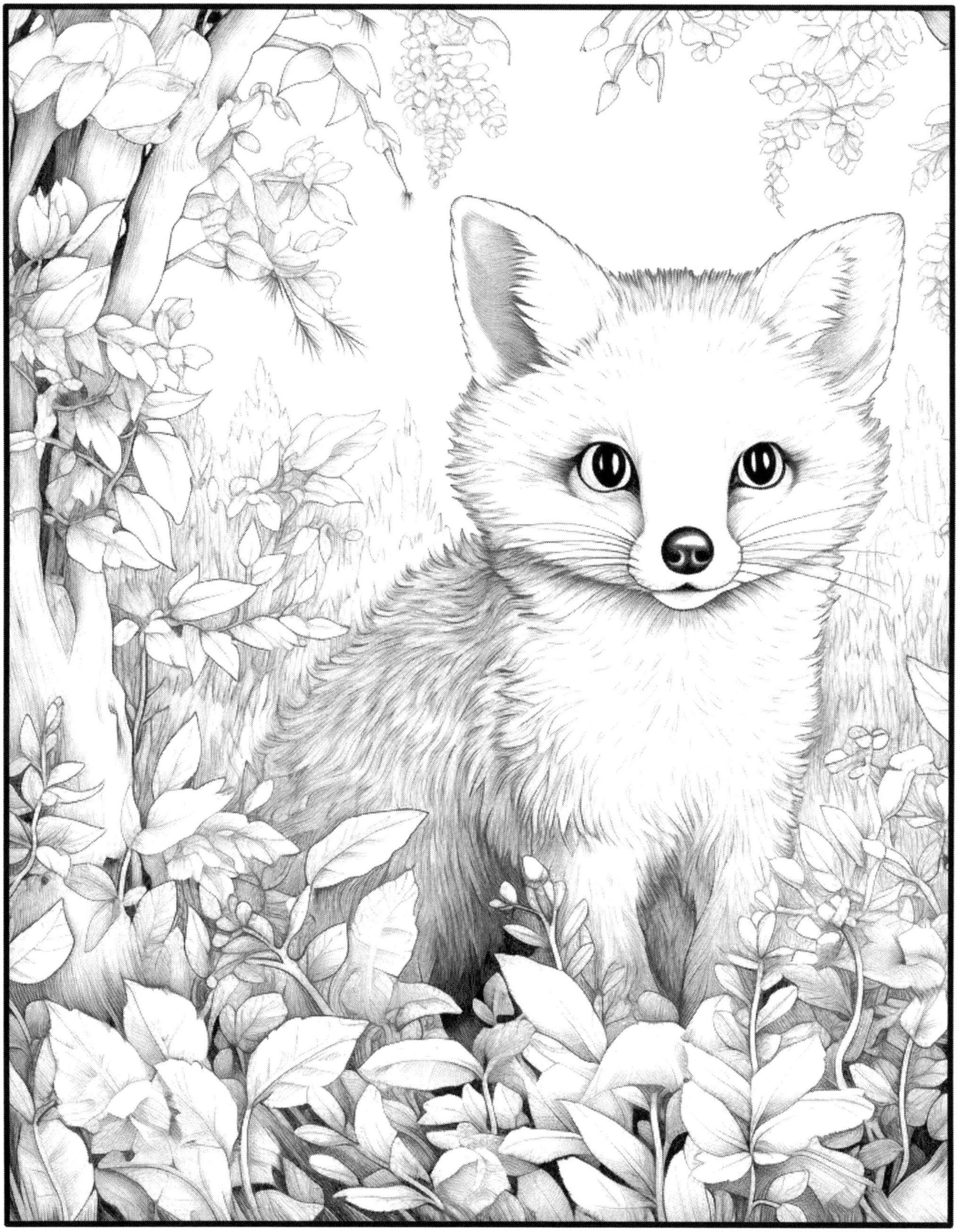

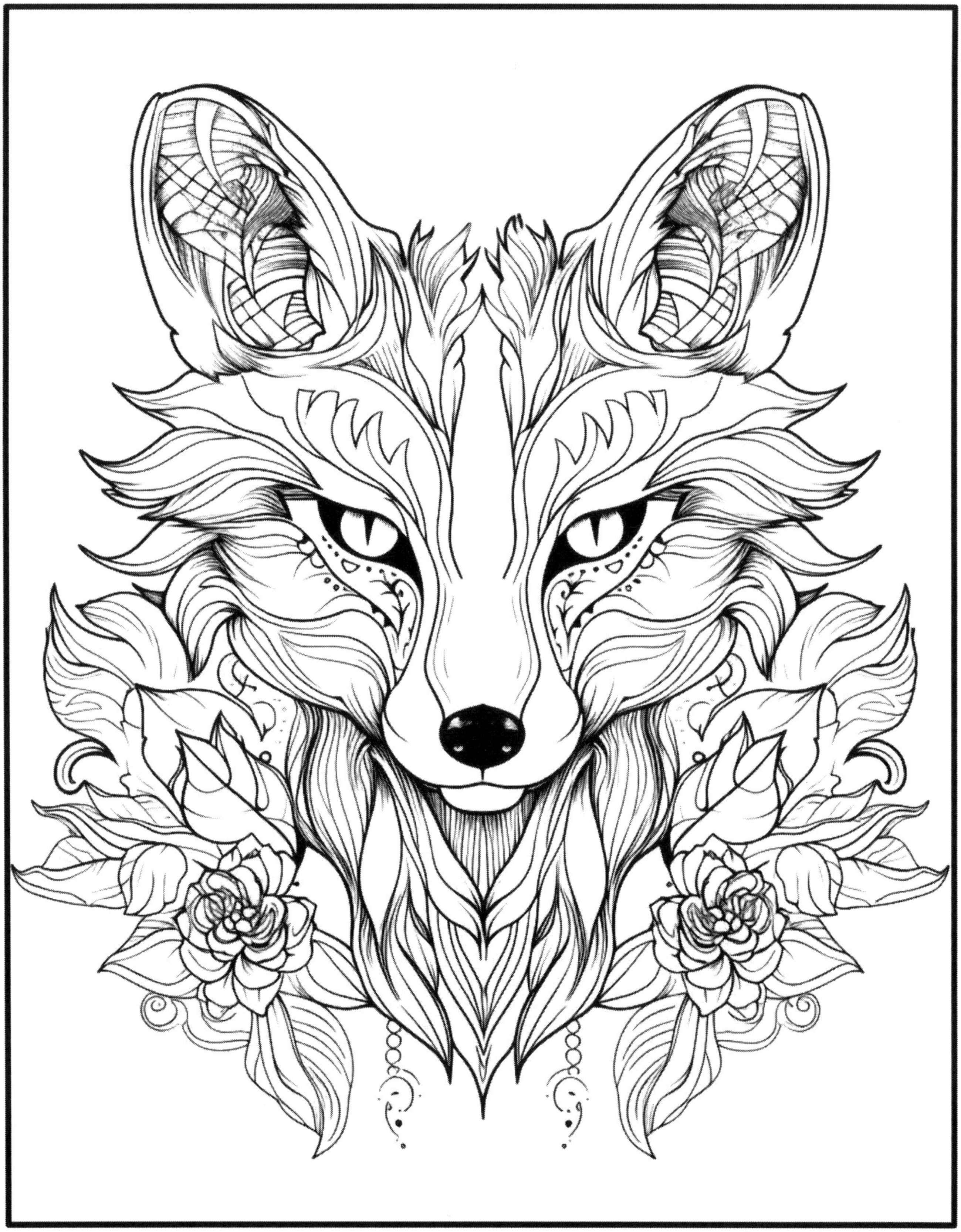

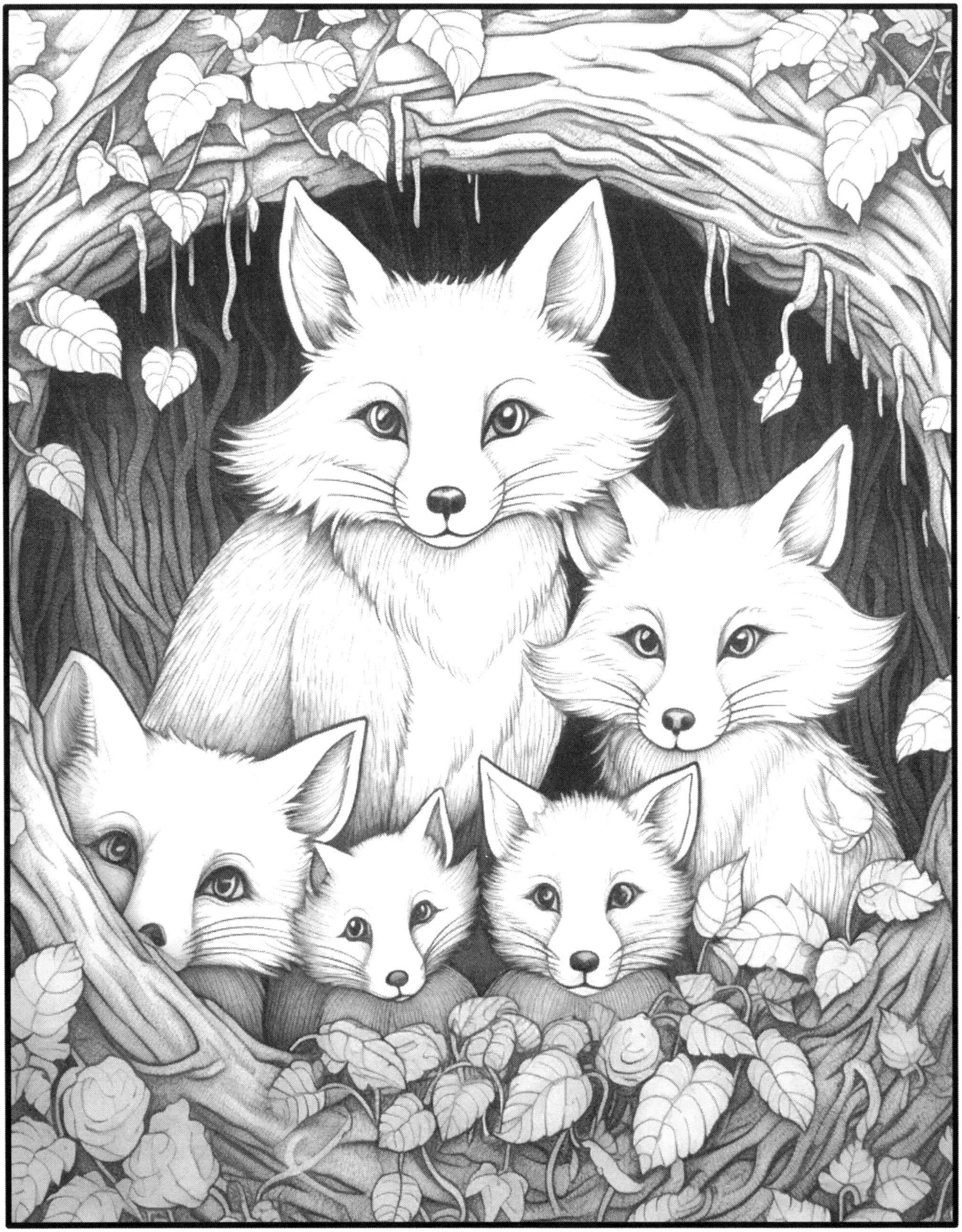

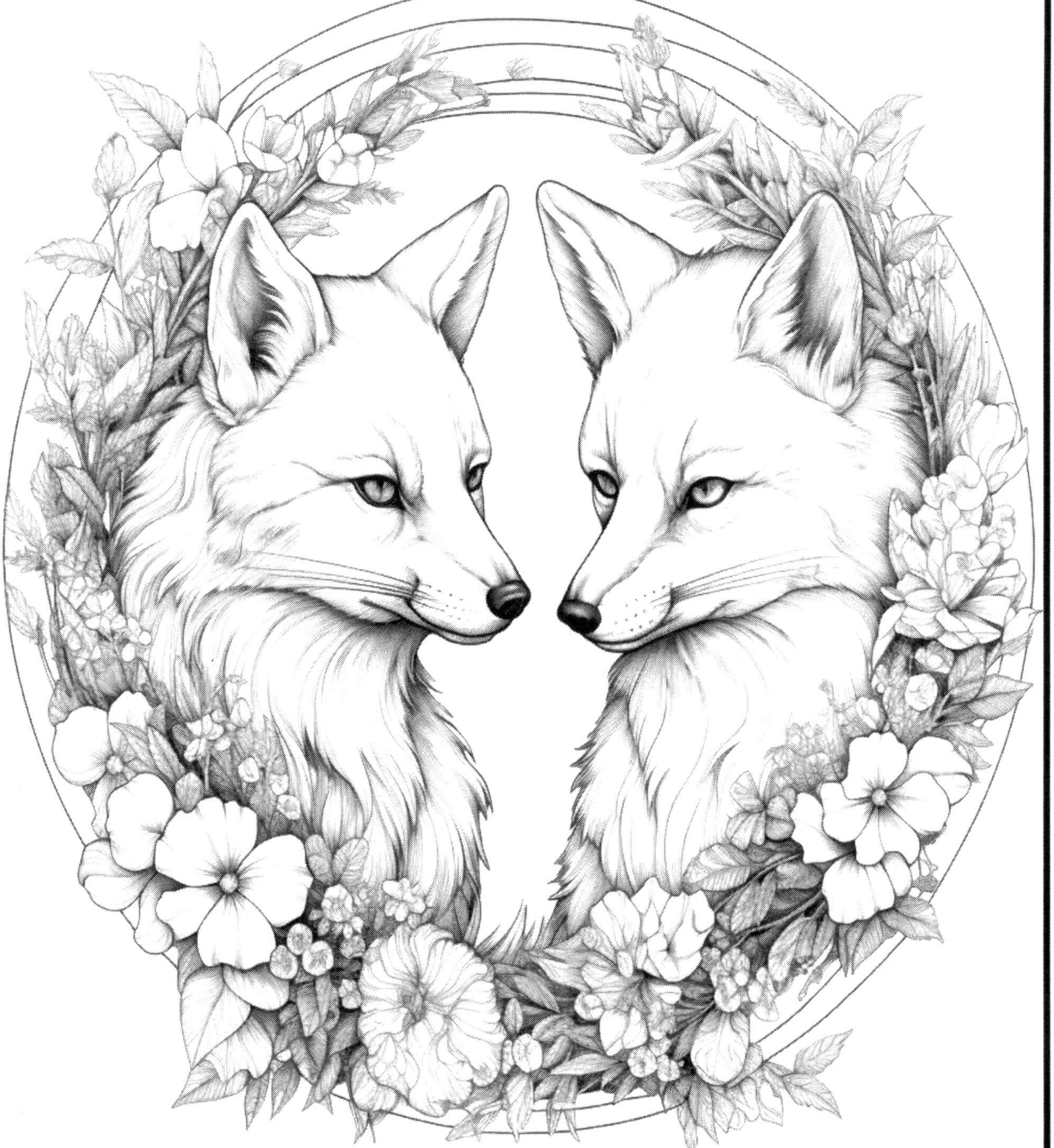

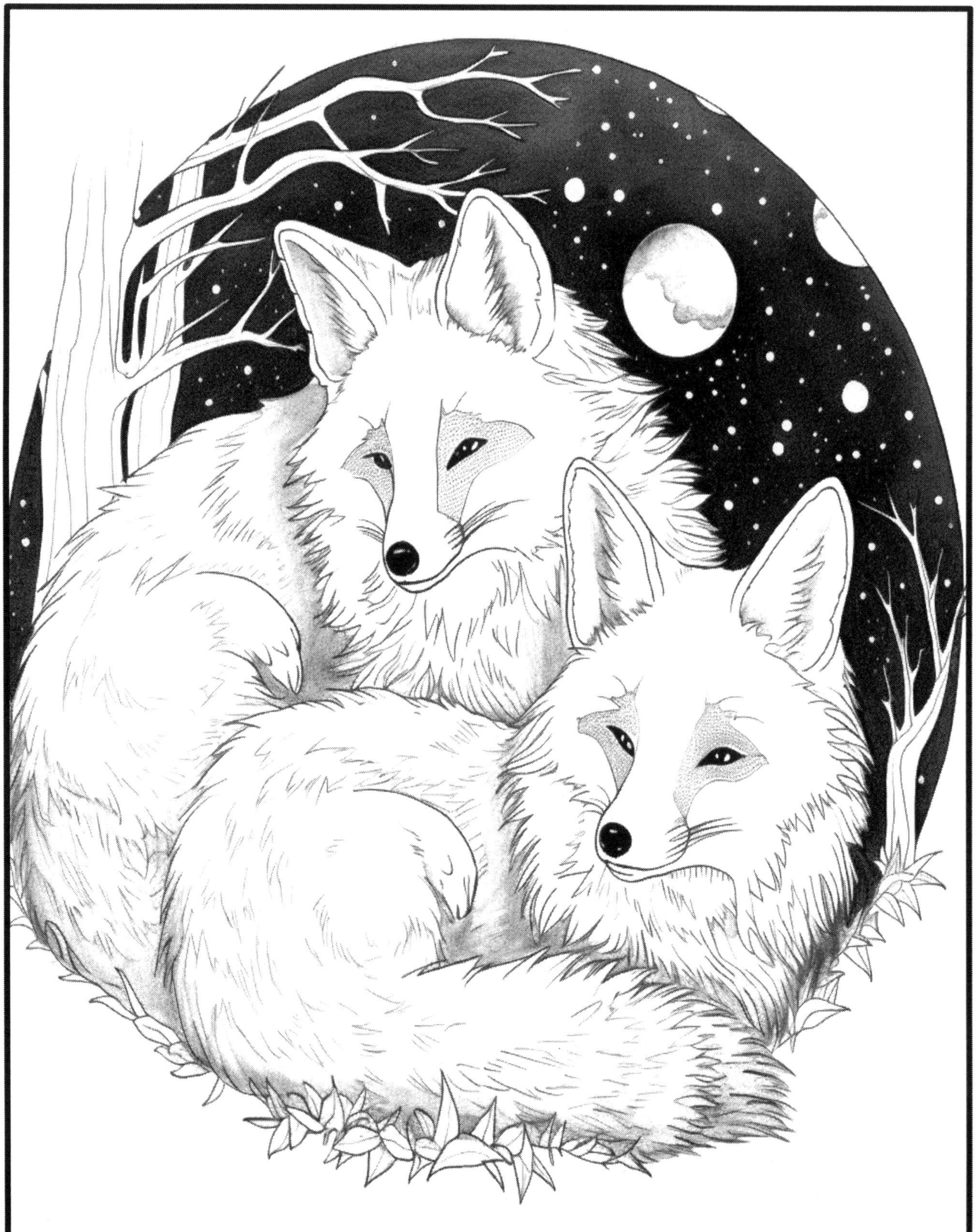

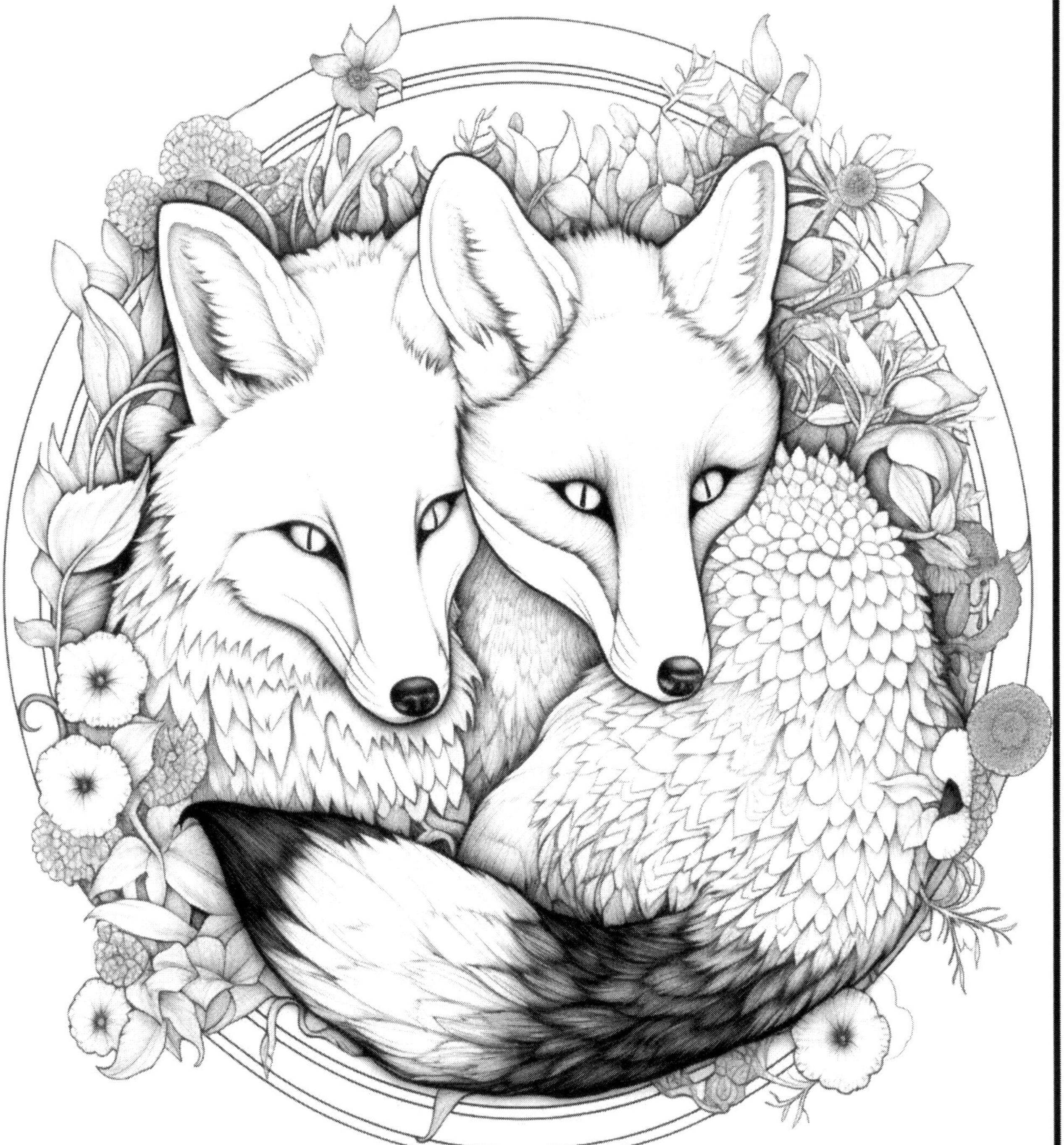

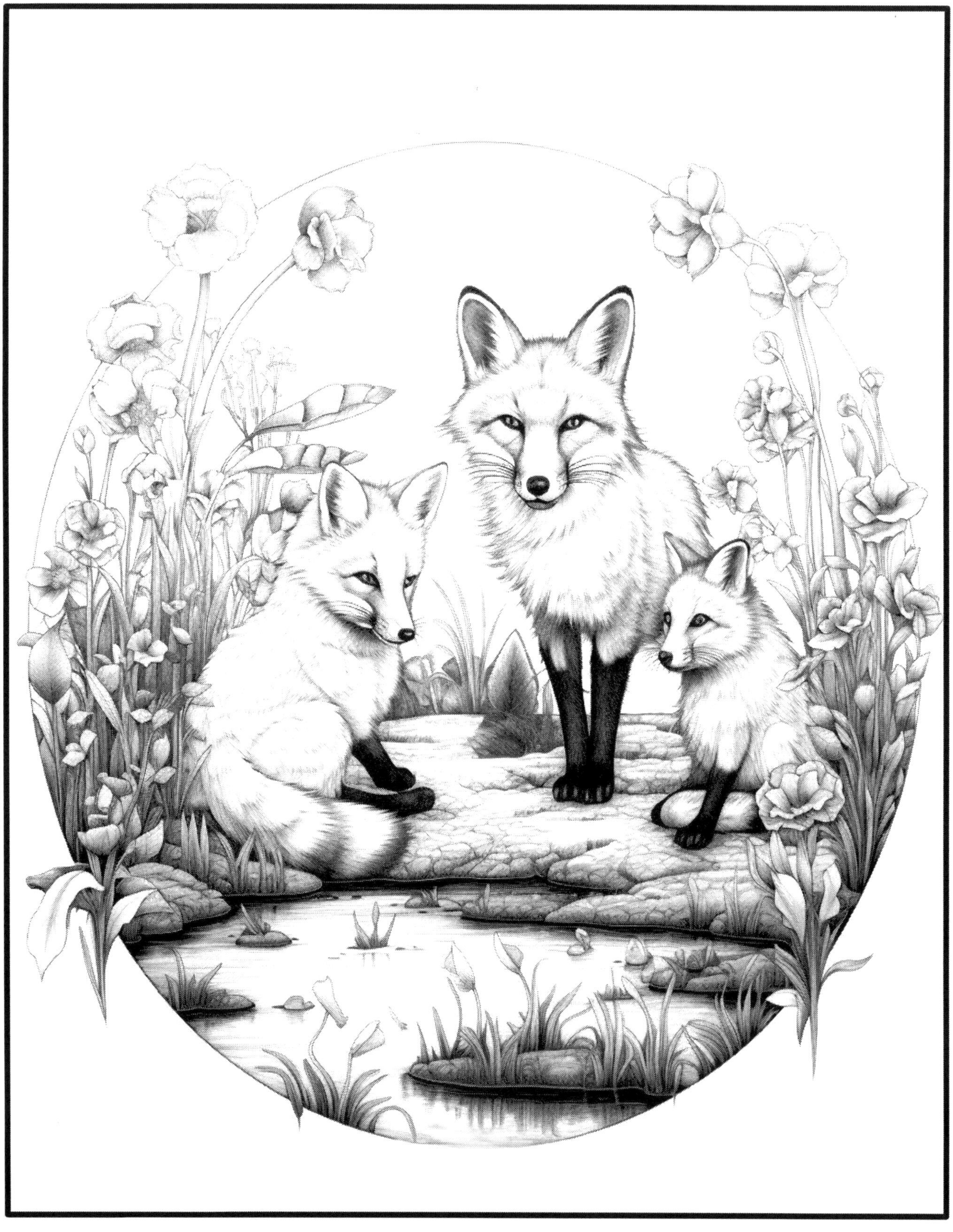

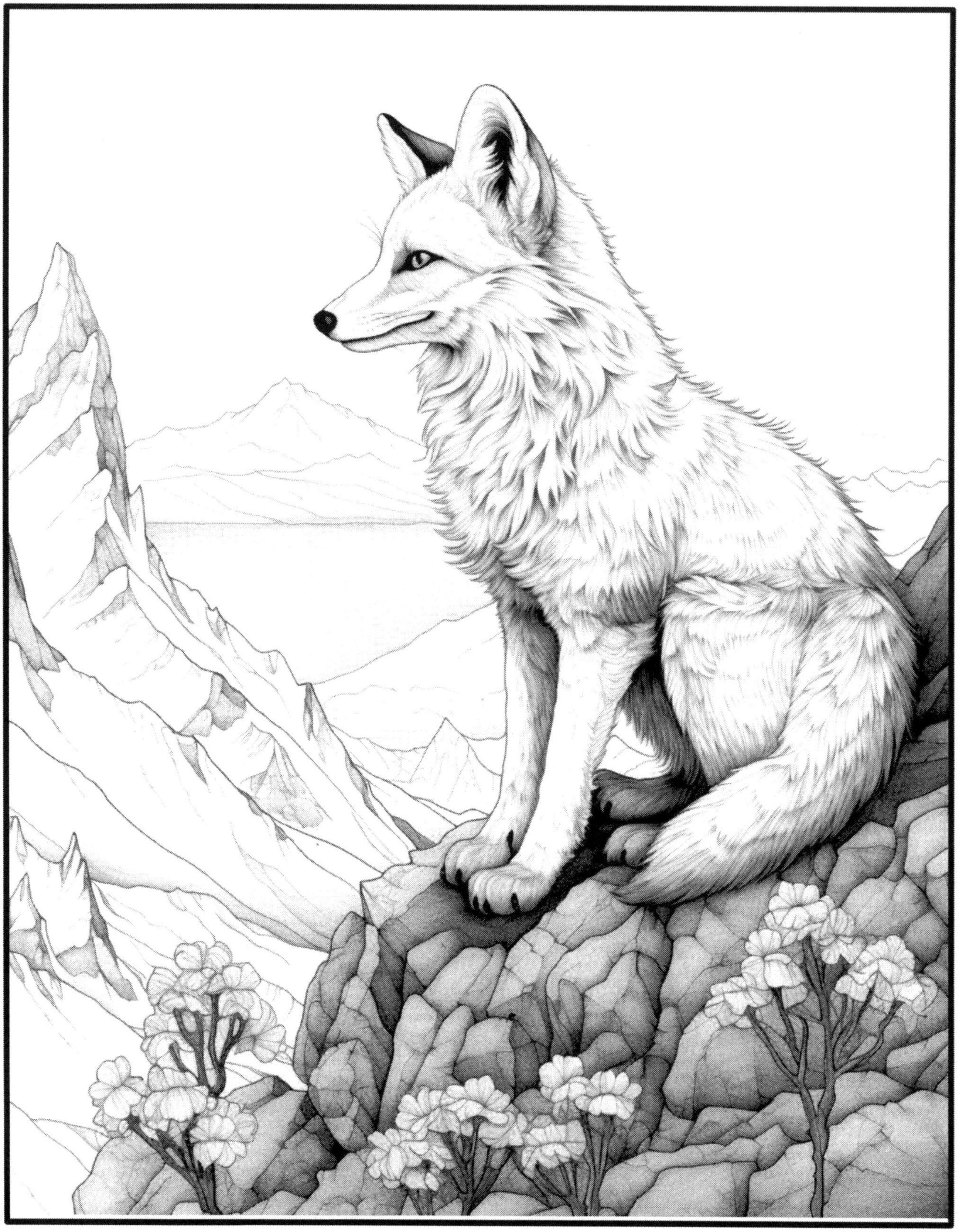

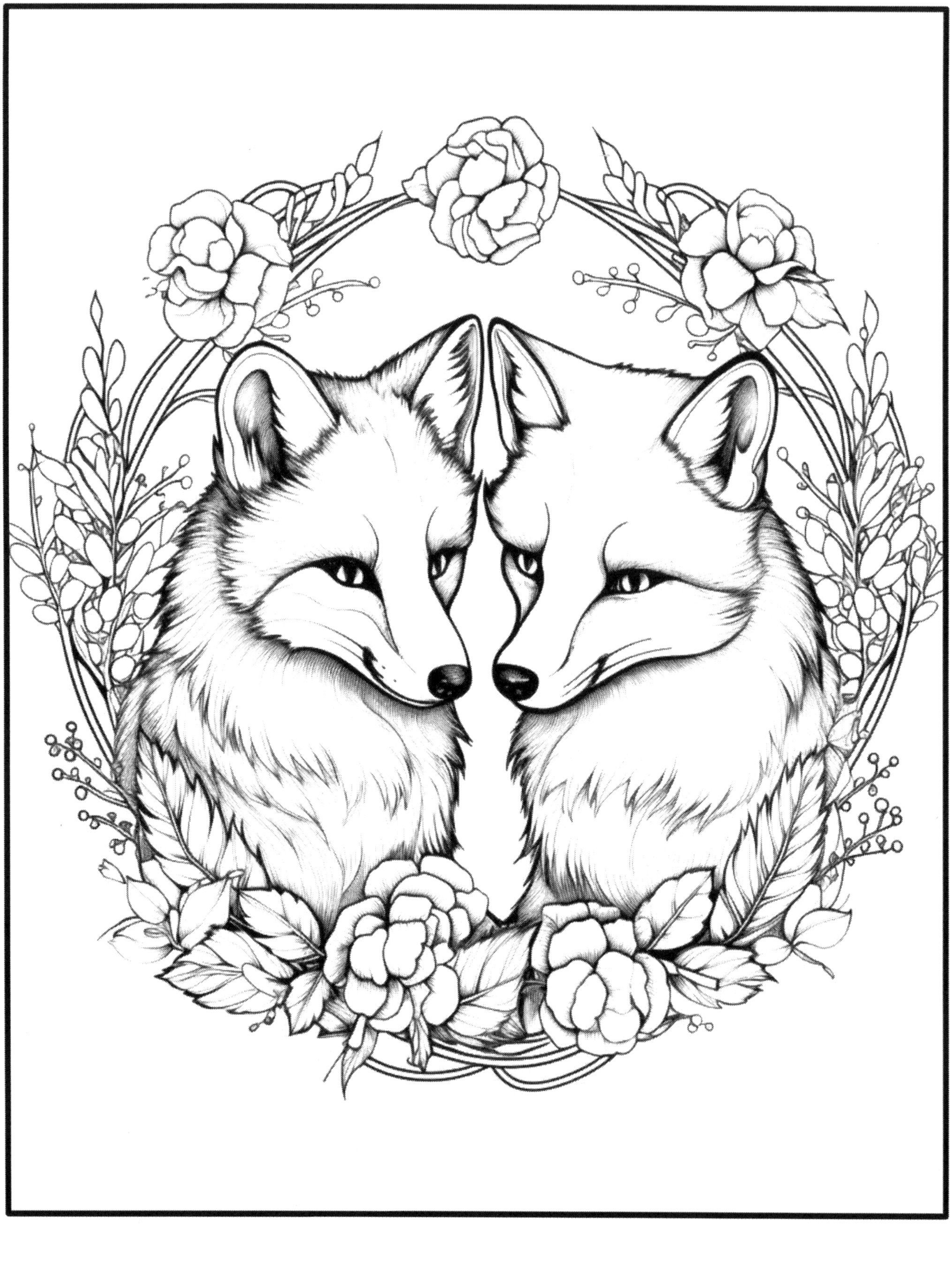

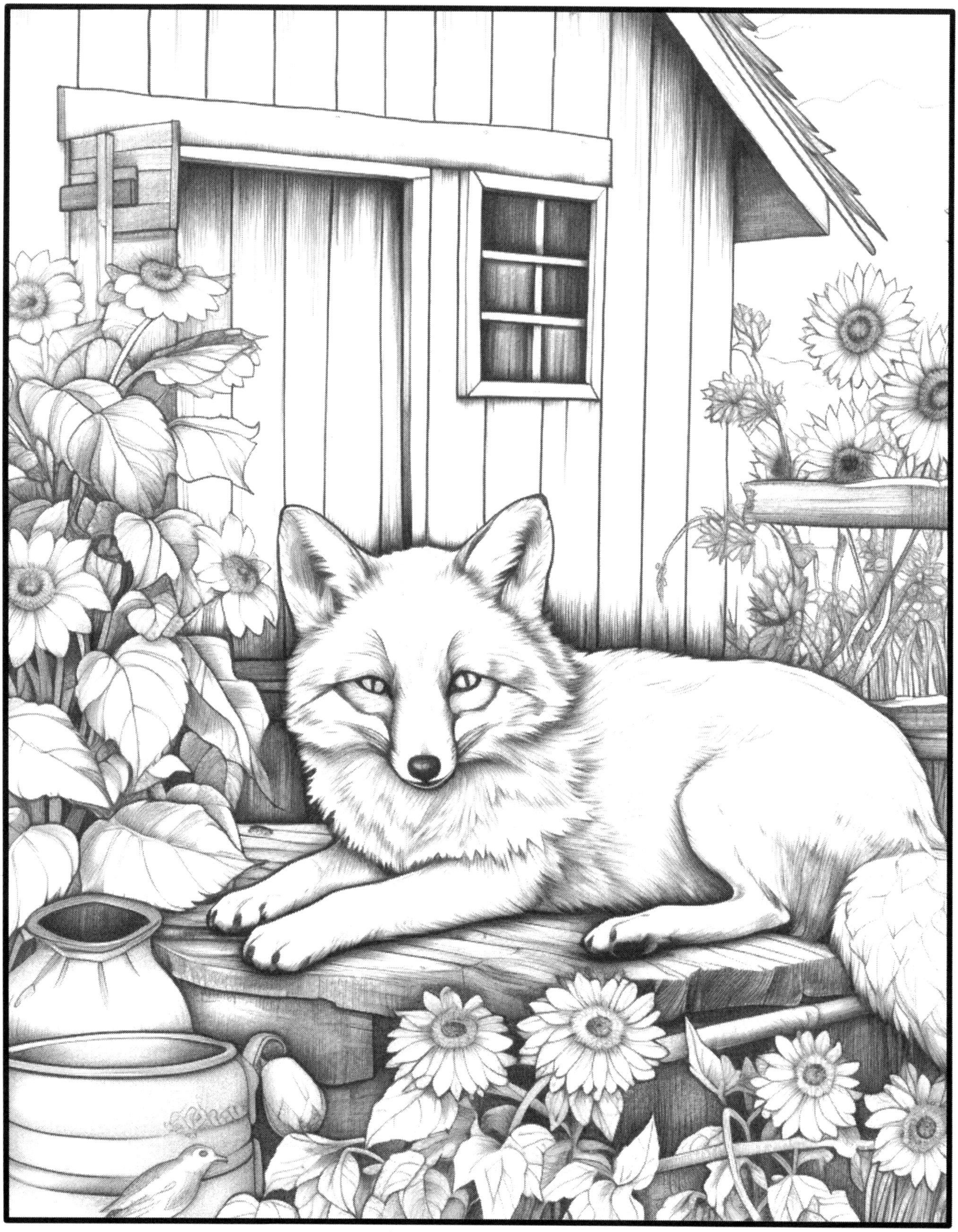

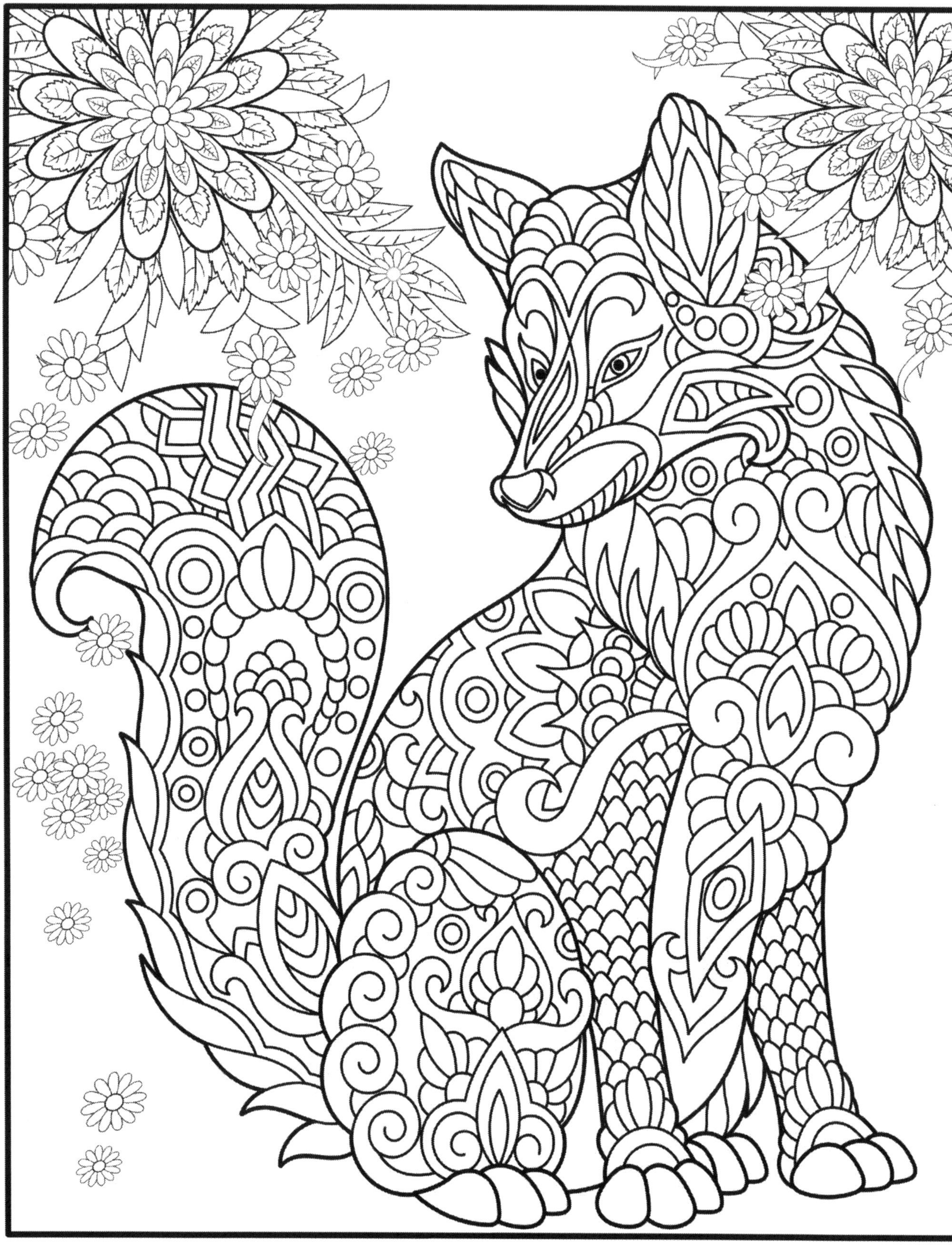

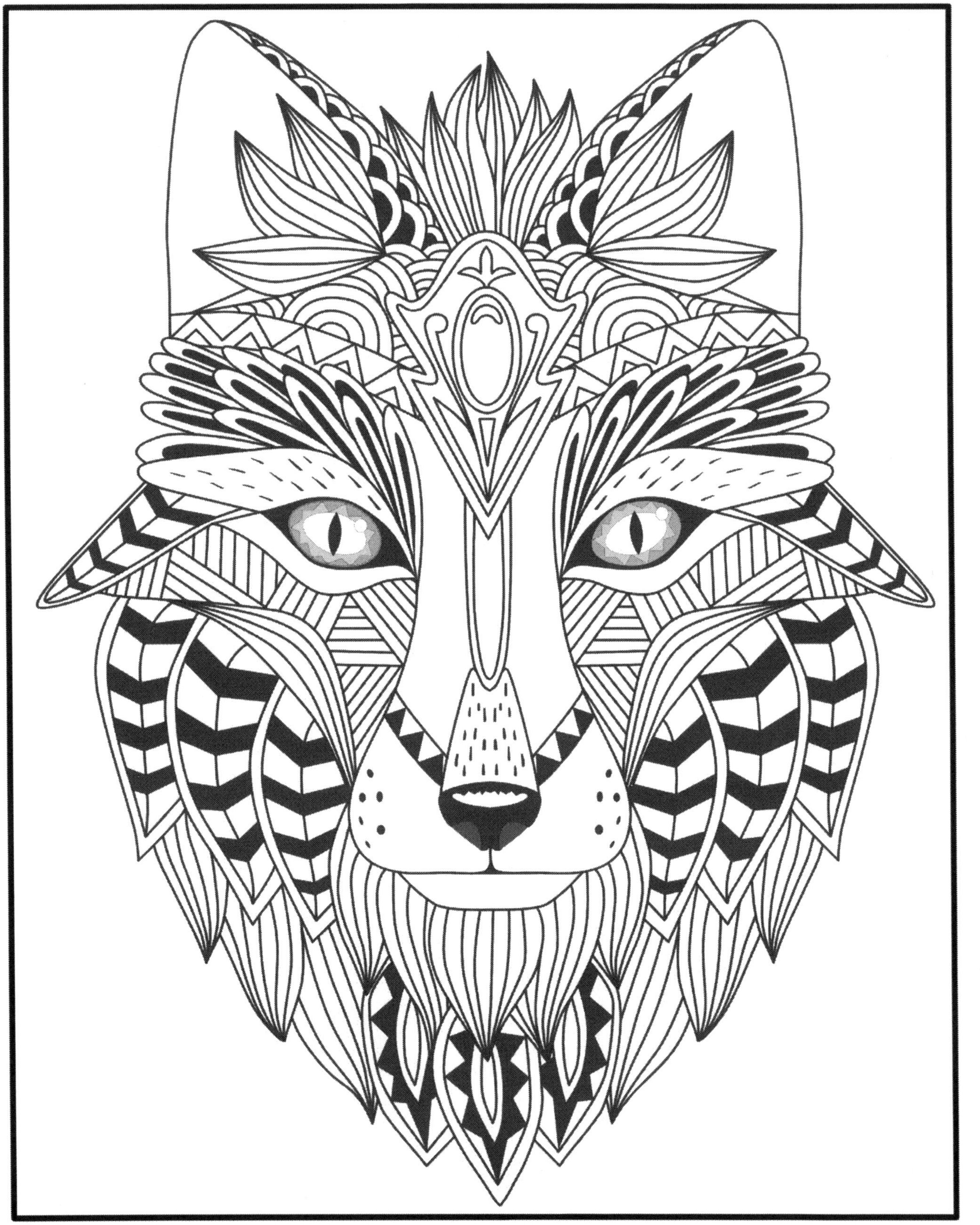

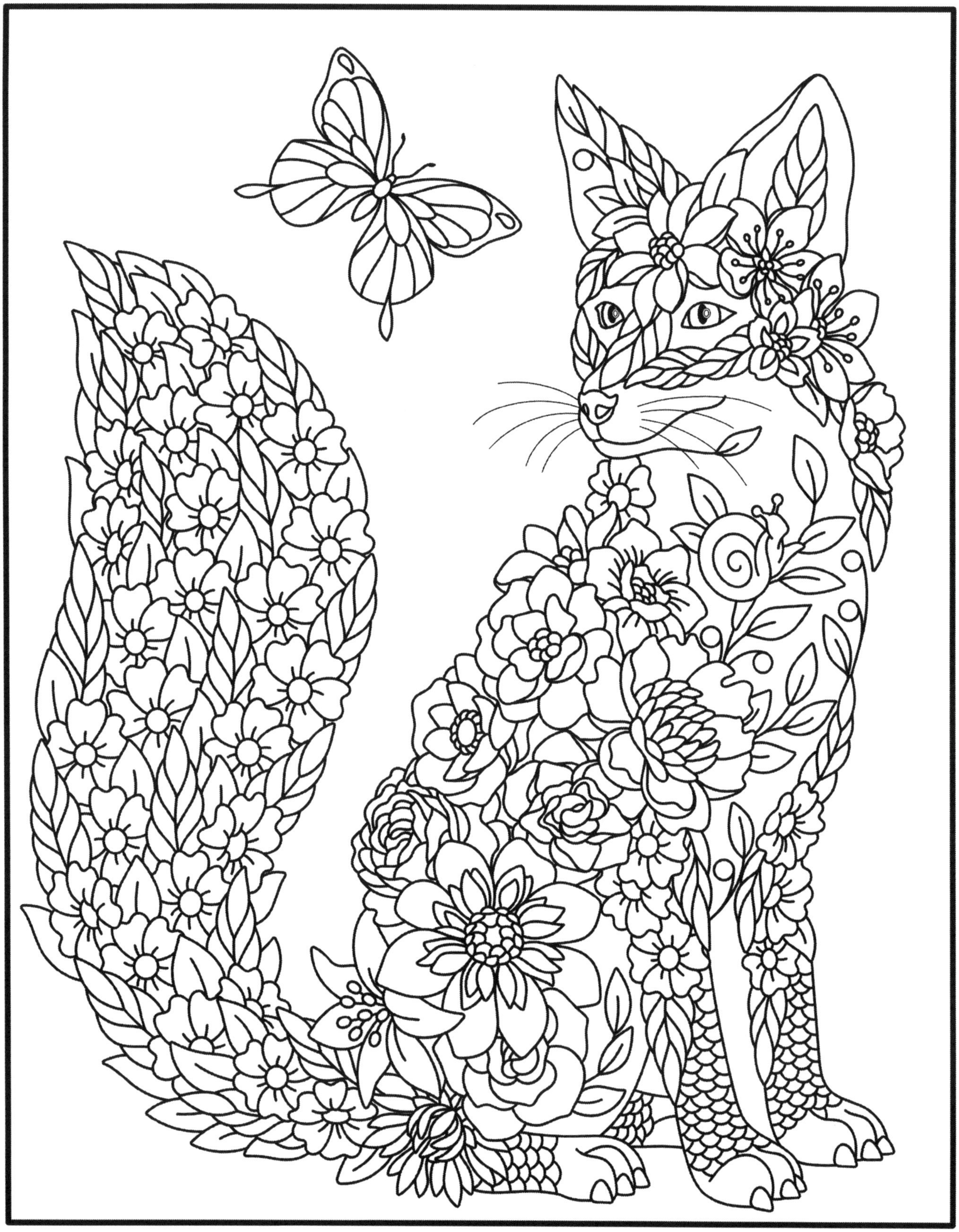

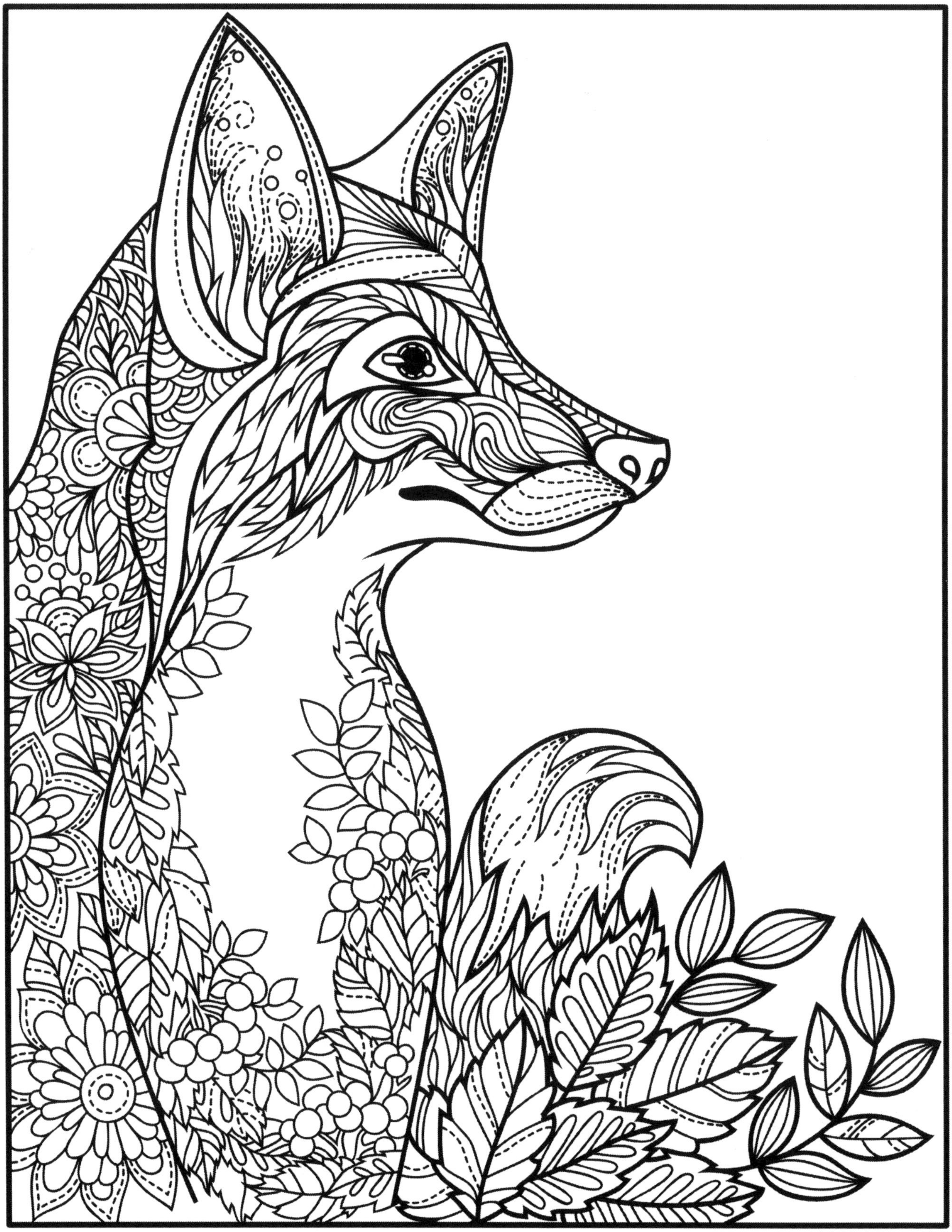

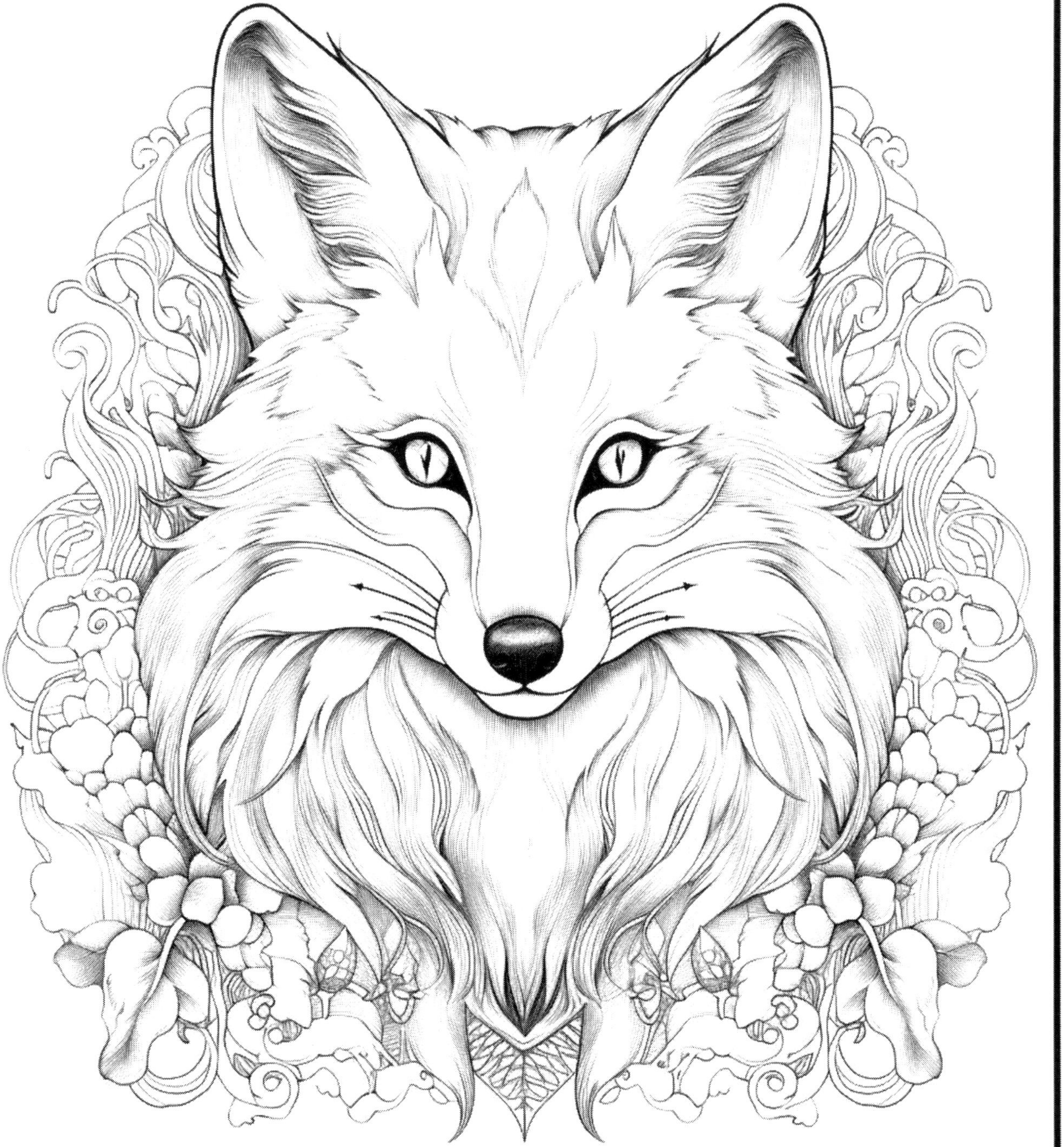

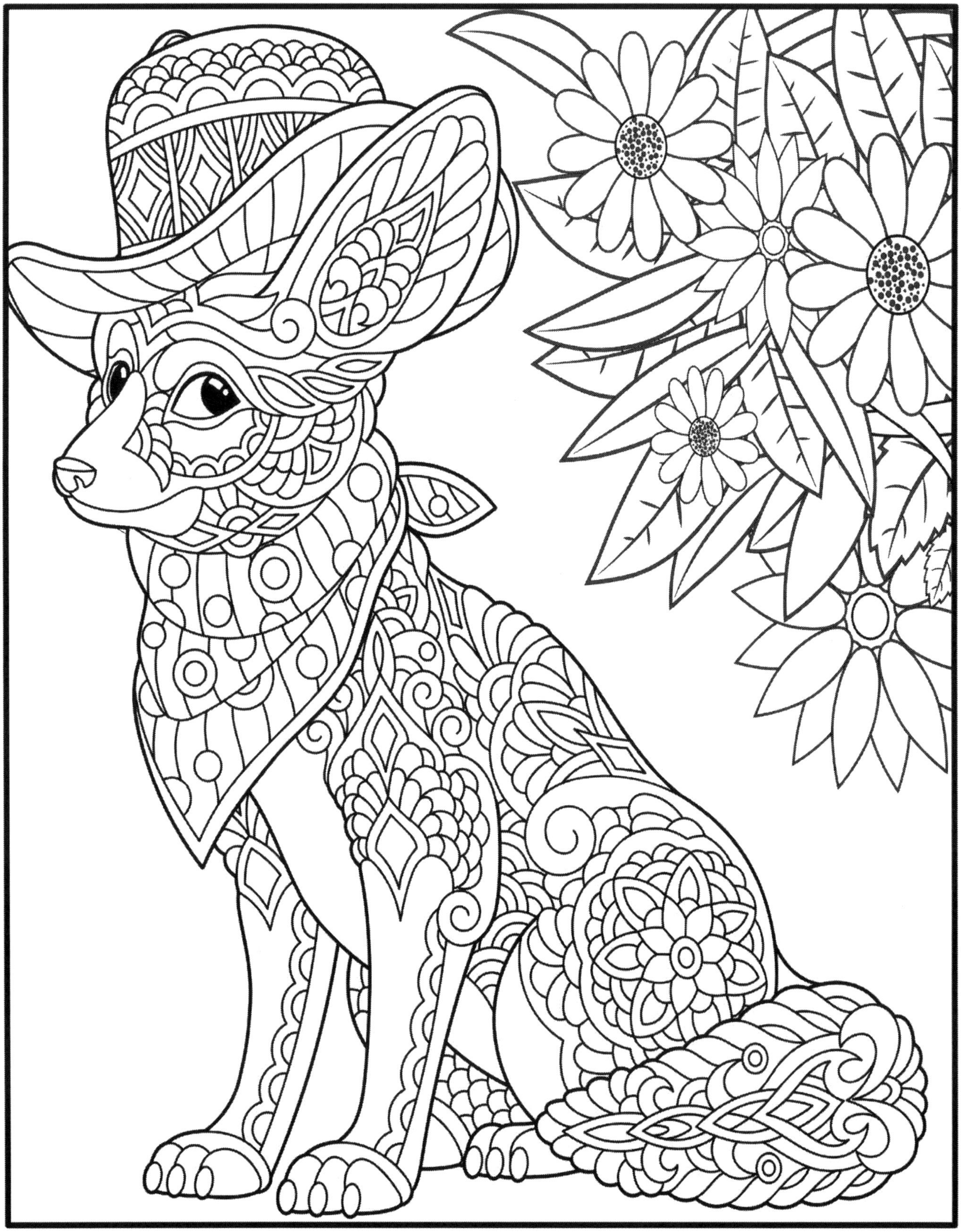

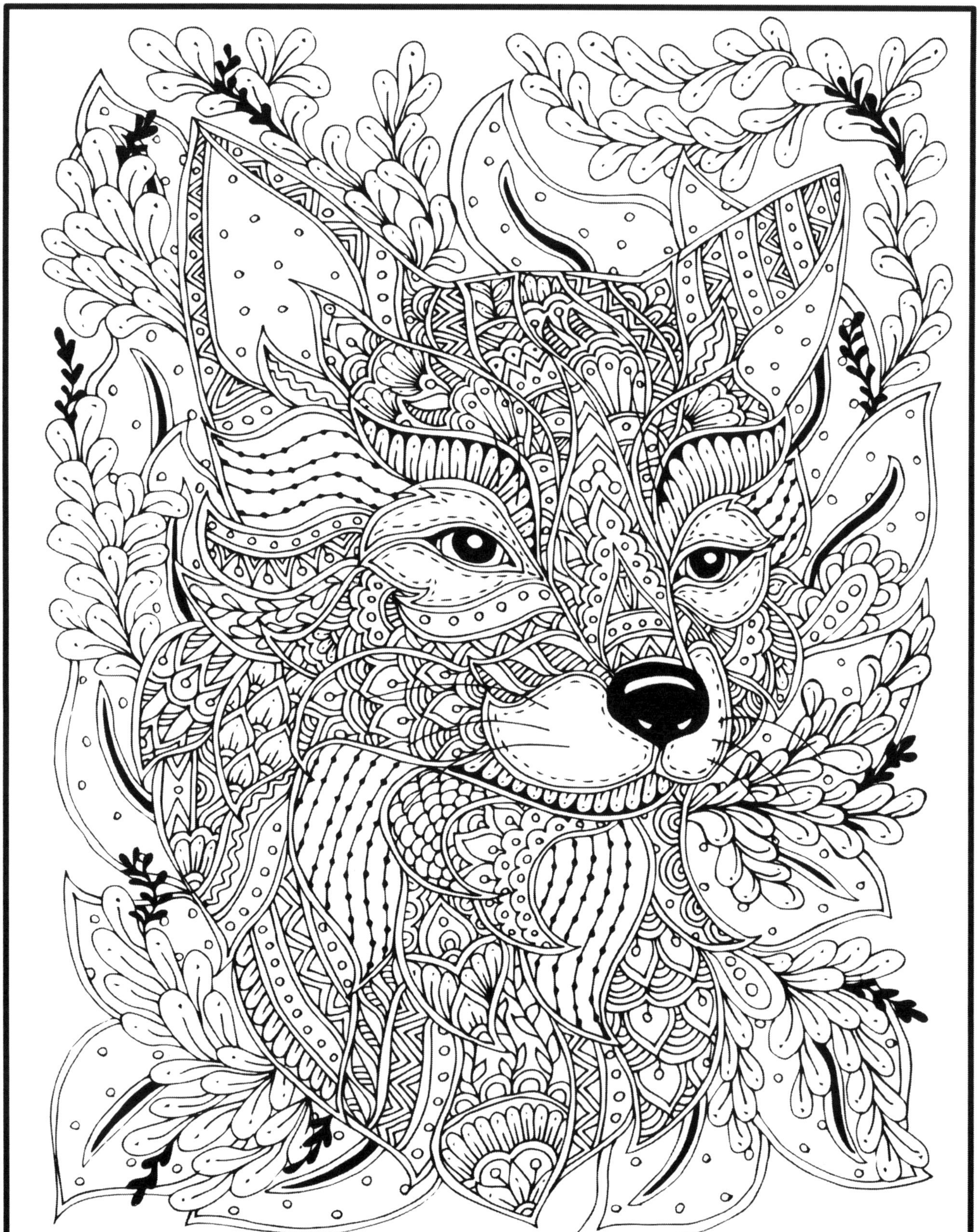

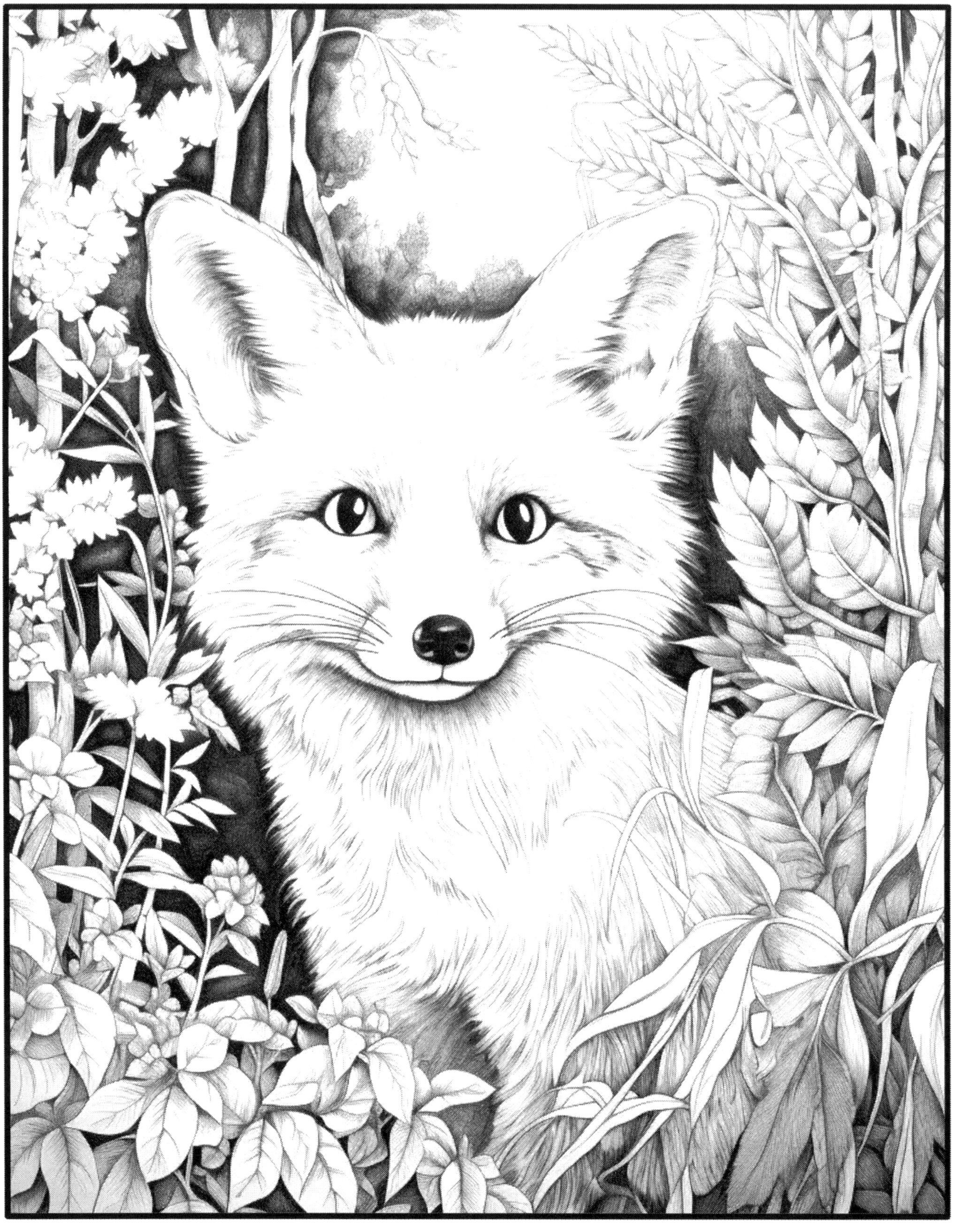

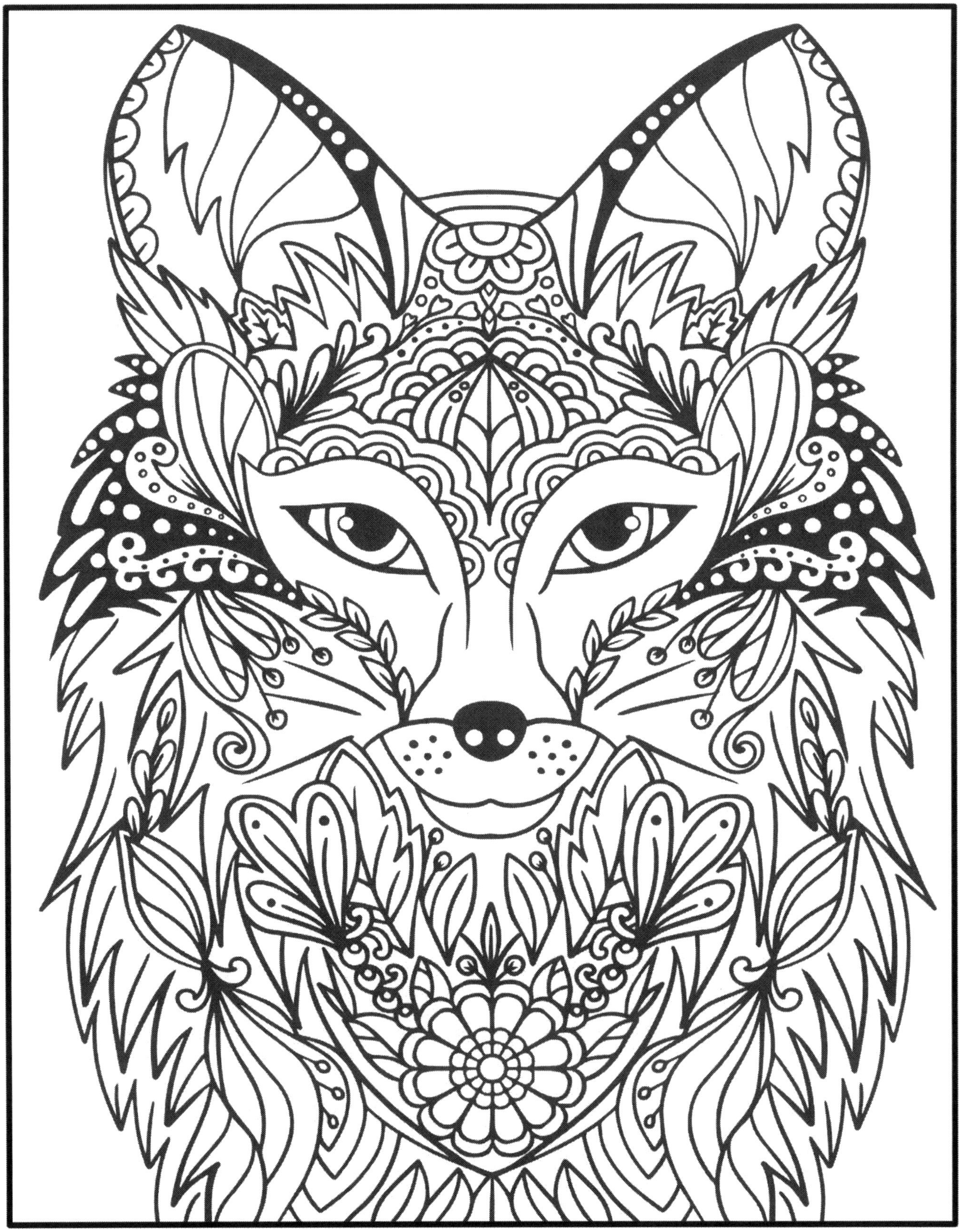

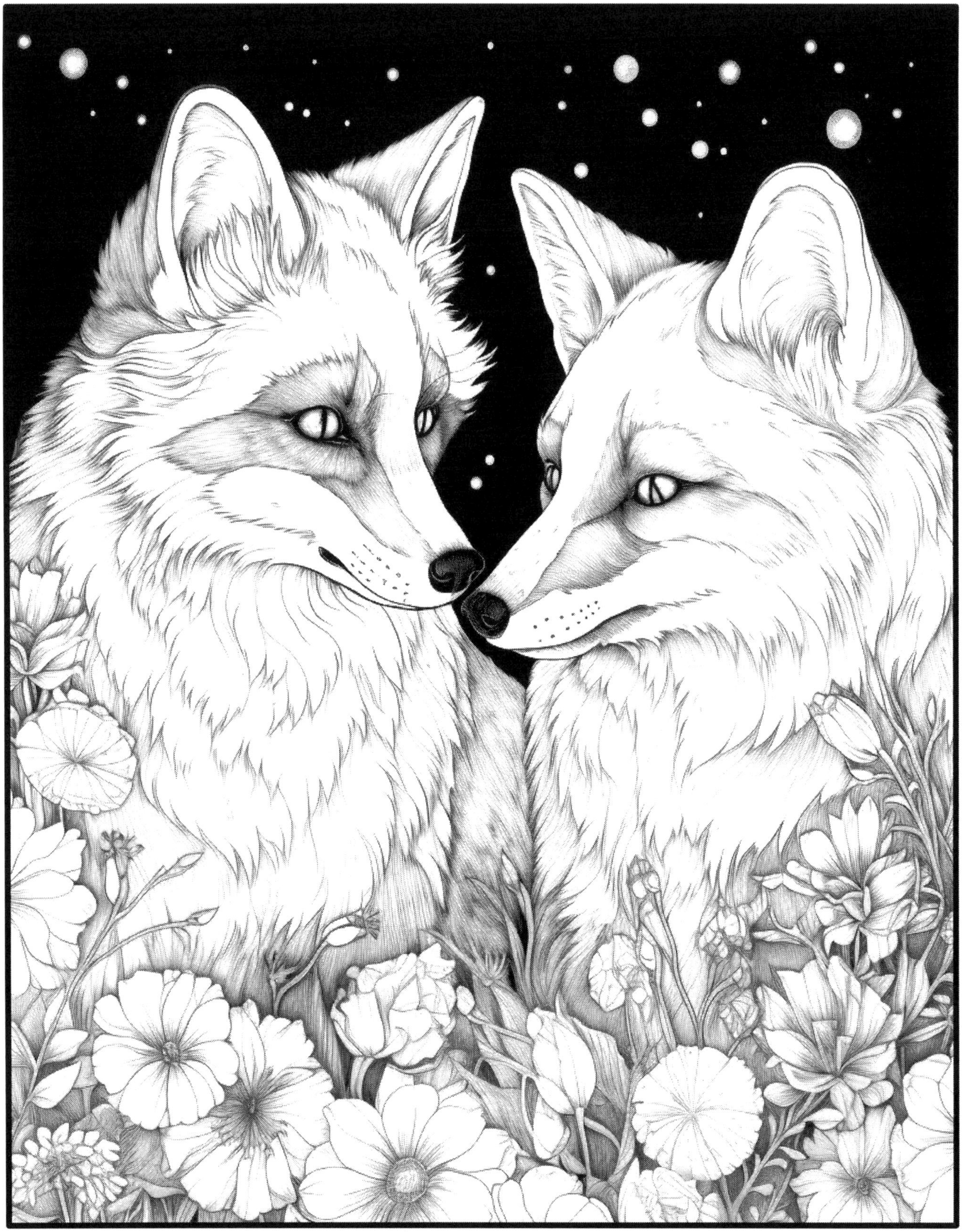

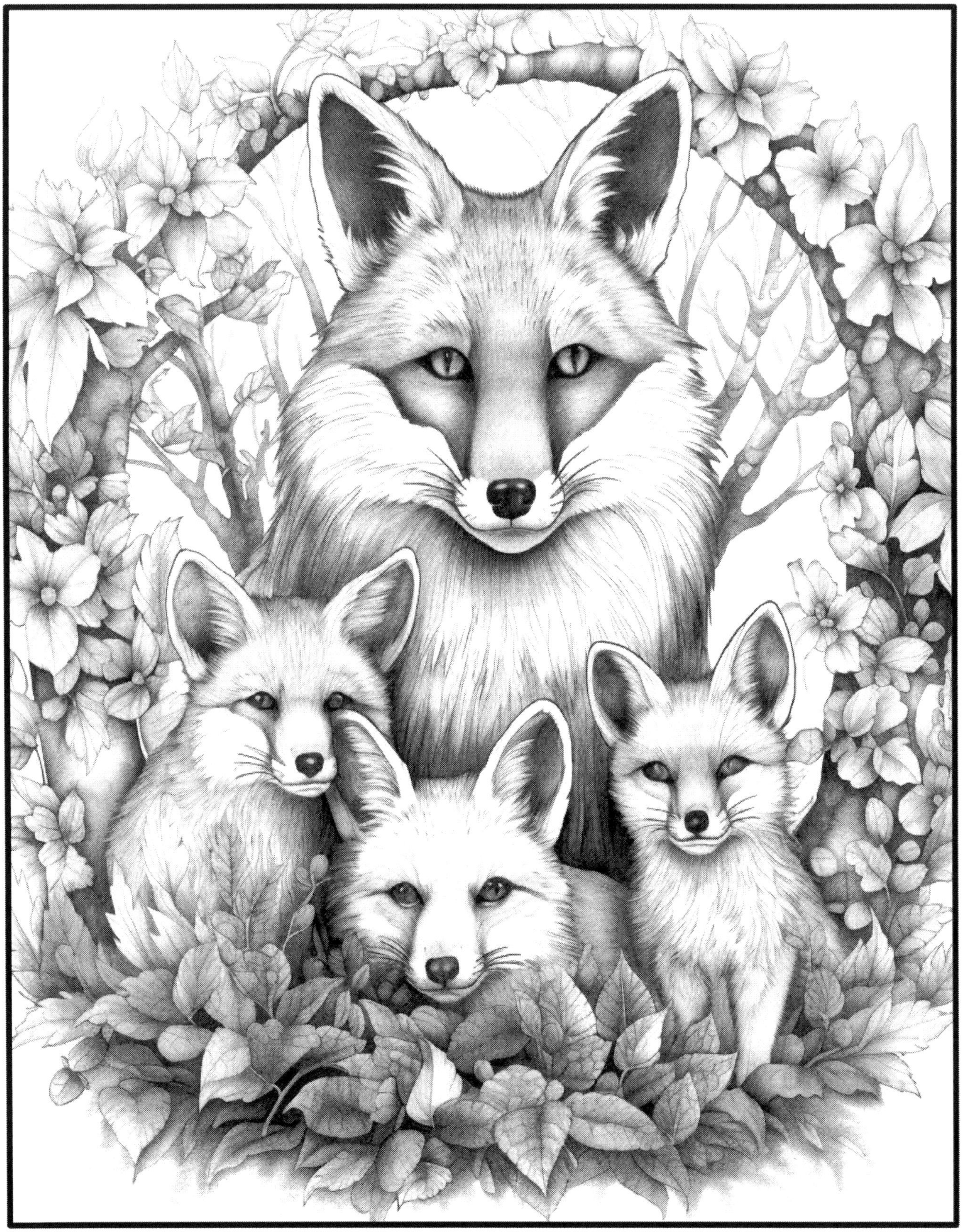

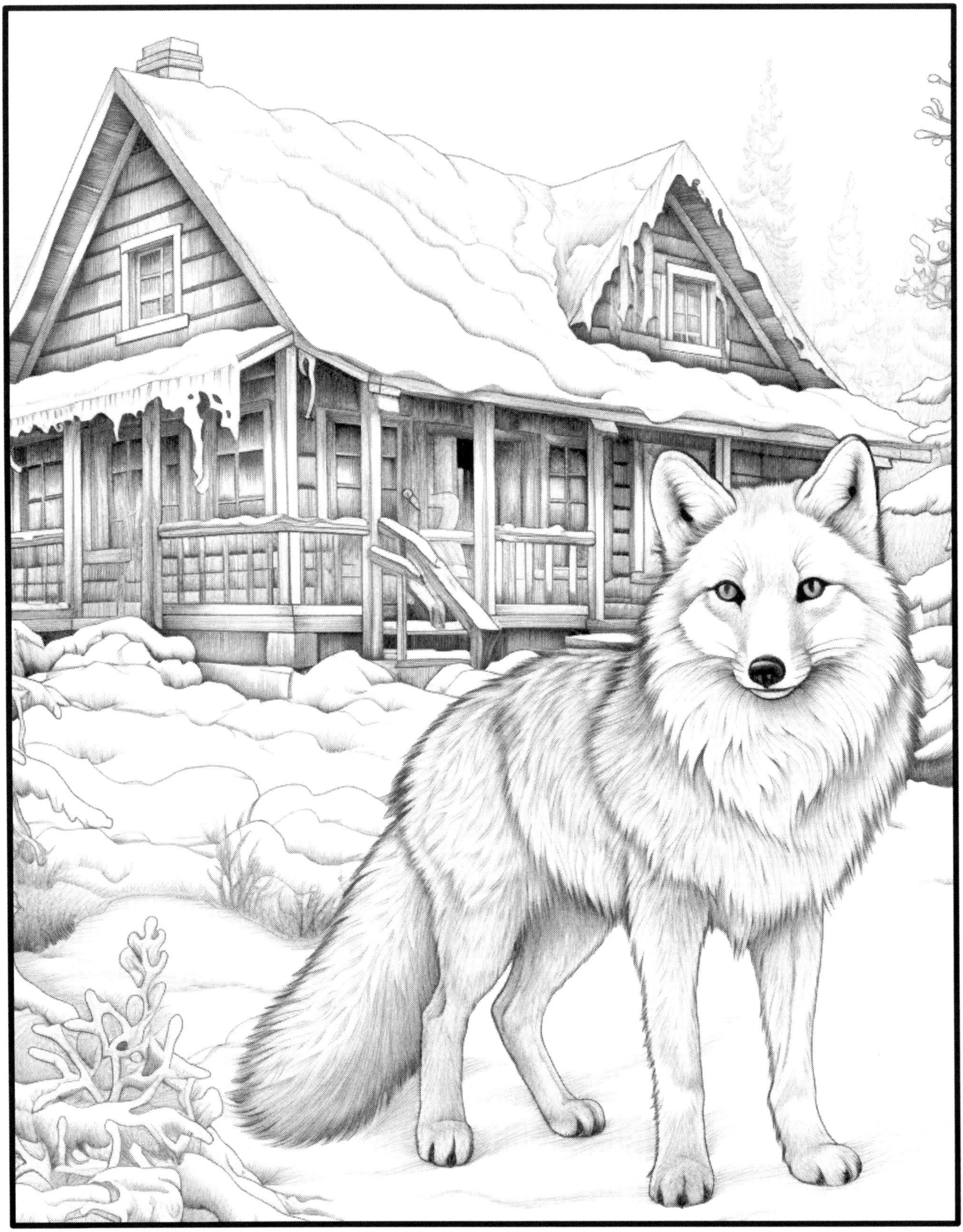

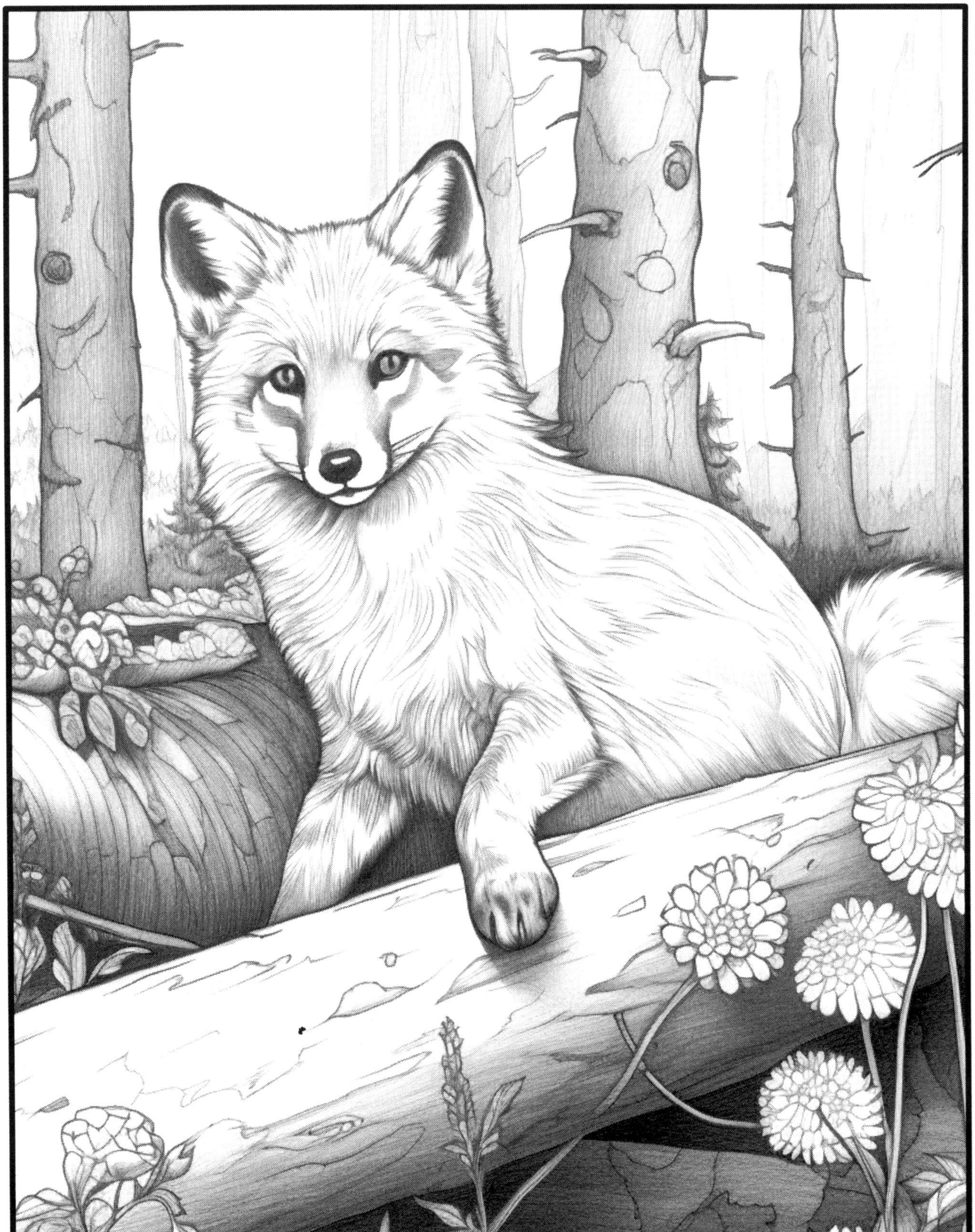

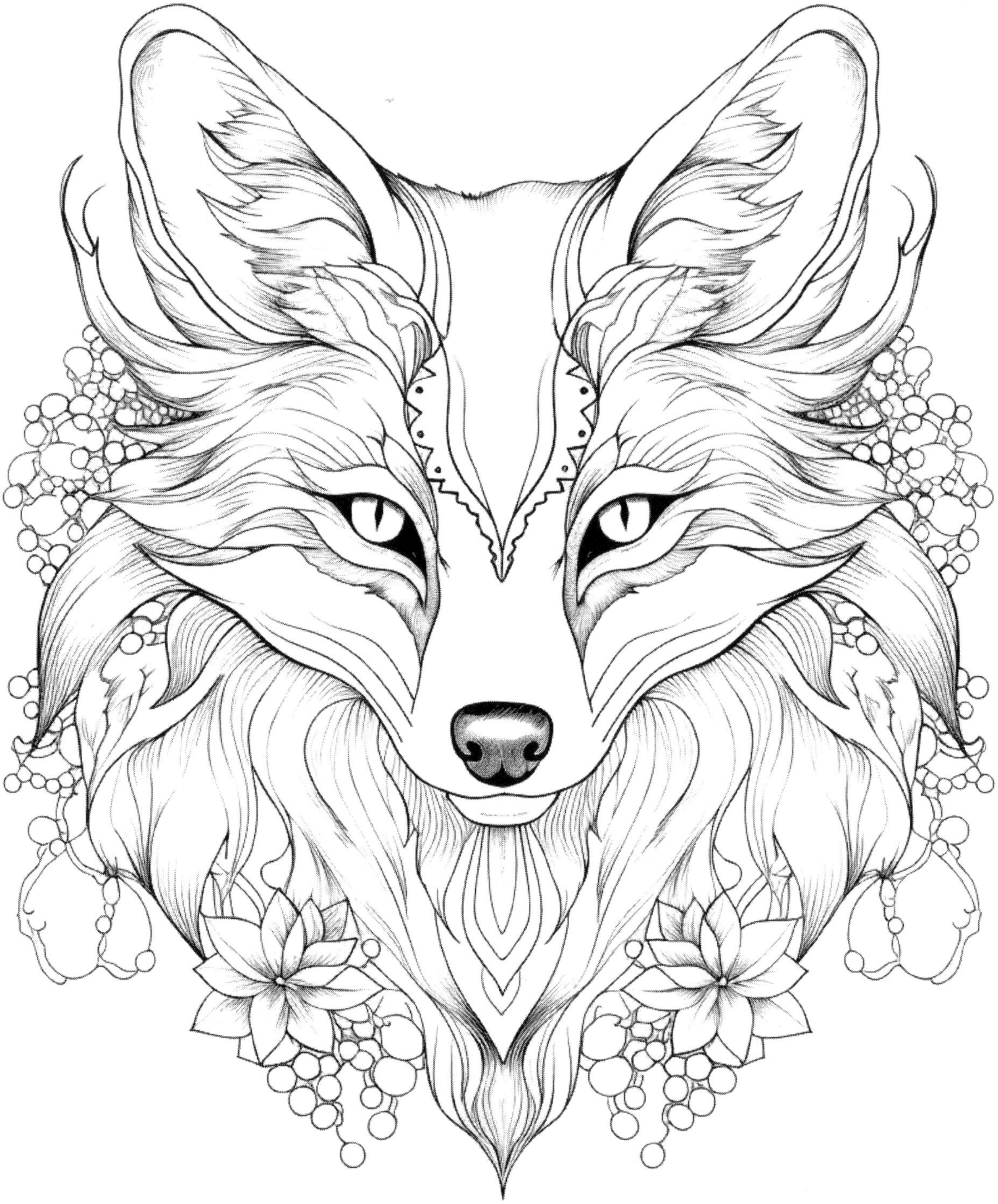

Made in the USA
Las Vegas, NV
23 December 2024

15114997R00050